The Sundance Choice Database

Flexible and valuable!

You select the readings … we provide your customized collection! Without a doubt, **The Sundance Choice Database** is the best way to provide your students with the reading selections that you want to teach—complete with rhetoric and writing instruction—at an ultimate value.

Featuring hundreds of classic and contemporary essay selections—chosen by English instructors from across the country—our unique database gives you the freedom to select only the essays or topics that fit your course. Each essay is surrounded by pedagogy that gets writing students engaged with the reading, and inspires them to do some original writing of their own.

A customized selection of readings made just for you!
The new *TextChoice* online system (**www.textchoice.com**) is the easiest and most flexible way to build your custom reader. Build your customized reader online, and receive a free evaluation copy!

It's never been easier to give your students an affordable, made-to-order collection of essays that you've designed . . . this PREVIEW and sample chapter will show you how.

An outstanding collection of resources—including our Comp21 CD-ROM—can accompany your adoption. See 6–8 for details.

Turn the page! Your brief tour starts now…

THOMSON
WADSWORTH

Preview

Sundance Choice

An Anthology of Readings

THOMSON
™
WADSWORTH

Australia · Canada · Mexico · Singapore · Spain · United Kingdom · United States

THOMSON
WADSWORTH

Sundance Choice
An Anthology of Readings

Custom Editor:
Mark Connelly

Project Development Editor:
Lori Peetz-Gud

Marketing Coordinator:
Lindsay Annett

Production/Manufacturing Supervisor:
Donna M. Brown

Sr. Project Coordinator:
Tina Esby

Pre-Media Services Supervisor:
Dan Plofchan

Rights and Permissions Specialist:
Bob Kauser

Senior Prepress Specialists:
Deanna Dixon

Cover Design:
Krista Pierson

Cover Image:
© Ross Anania/Getty Images

For information about our products, contact us at:
Thomson Learning Academic Resource Center
(800) 423-0563

For permission to use material from this text or product, submit a request online at
http://www.thomsonrights.com.
Any additional questions about permissions can be submitted by email to
thomsonrights@thomson.com.

The Adaptable Courseware Program consists of products and additions to existing Wadsworth products that are produced from camera-ready copy. Peer review, class testing, and accuracy are primarily the responsibility of the author(s).

Student Edition: ISBN

Thomson Custom Solutions
5191 Natorp Boulevard
Mason, OH 45040
www.thomsoncustom.com

Thomson Higher Education
10 Davis Drive
Belmont, CA 94002-3098 USA

Asia (Including India):
Thomson Learning
60 Albert Street, #15-01
Albert Complex
Singapore 189969
Tel 65 336-6411
Fax 65 336-7411

Australia/New Zealand:
Thomson Learning Australia
102 Dodds Street
Southbank, Victoria 3006
Australia

Latin America:
Thomson Learning
Seneca 53
Colonia Polano
11560 Mexico, D.F., Mexico
Tel (525) 281-2906
Fax (525) 281-2656

Canada:
Thomson Nelson
1120 Birchmount Road
Toronto, Ontario
Canada M1K 5G4
Tel (416) 752-9100
Fax (416) 752-8102

UK/Europe/Middle East/Africa:
Thomson Learning
High Holborn House
50-51 Bedford Row
London, WC1R 4L$
United Kingdom
Tel 44 (020) 7067-2500
Fax 44 (020) 7067-2600

Spain (Includes Portugal):
Thomson Paraninfo
Calle Magallanes 25
28015 Madrid
España
Tel 34 (0)91 446-3350
Fax 34 (0)91 445-6218

Outstanding pedagogical tools and visual aids that draw students into each selection

Every reading in The **Sundance Choice Database** engages and inspires through pedagogical tools and features—soon, your students are sure to begin original writing of their own!

Unlike any other custom database, **The Sundance Choice Database** offers full coverage of rhetoric, presenting topics that will benefit beginning writers as well as topics more appropriate for experienced writers. Additionally, a **model student paper** is included in each theme or mode, to give your students an idea of comparable writing.

Evaluating Strategy

1. What tone is established in the first sentence? What does the use of the word *victim* indicate?
2. Rendón includes a quote from one of his articles. Is this an effective device?
3. *BLENDING THE MODES.* How does Rendón use narration, description, and comparison in developing "Kiss of Death"?

Appreciating Language

1. What does the term "kiss of death" mean to you? Do you associate it with the Bible or with Hollywood images of the Mafia?
2. Rendón uses several Spanish words without providing definitions in English. What does this suggest about his idea of the United States becoming "acculturized" to Mexican-American culture?
3. Rendón uses both "Mexican-American" and "Chicano." What definitions of these terms are you familiar with? Do "Latino" and "Hispanic" have different meanings and connotations?

by "cautious Chicanos"?

ng Suggestions

of death" you have escaped in your own
omised your future by taking

STUDENT PAPER

No Deterrence

1   Does the death penalty deter anyone? One of the main arguments people use to support capital punishment is deterrence—the idea that seeing someone executed will make others think before committing a similar crime. In theory it might have that effect. If a gang member murdered a police officer or shot up a liquor store and killed six people, maybe executing him within a year of conviction might influence other gang members and younger people who admired him.

2   But today people spend years, sometimes decades, on death row before being executed. Stays and appeals delay executions to the point that any deterrent factor is lost. When a 38-year-old man is executed for a crime he committed when he was 25, who will be deterred? No doubt his gang no longer exists. The current generation of young criminals can't relate to him and don't see his fate connected to theirs. In addition, whatever shock and horror people felt by an outrageous crime has long worn off. Executing someone years after the crime becomes only an afterthought, a minor news item. Any deterrent power is long gone.

Within each theme or mode, two **images** are available for selection. Each visual within the image bank is accompanied by questions, writing assignments, and collaborative activities.

Responding to Images

Responding to Images

Sojourner Truth, *Ain't I a Woman?* ▪ Bruno Bettleheim, *The Holocaust* ▪ Nancy Gibbs, *When Is It Rape?* ▪ Michael Dorris, *Fetal Alcohol Syndrome* ▪ George Orwell, *A Hanging* ▪ Edward Koch, *Death and Justice: How Capital Punishment Affirms Life* ▪ Daniel Lashof, *Earth's Last Gasp?* ▪ Joycelyn Tomkin, *Hot Air* ▪ Anna Quindlen, *Horrors: Girls With Gavels! What A Difference a Day Makes. And If the Boys Stay Home—Well, There's a Lesson There, Too* ▪ Judith Viorst, *Bones Break, But Boys Endure* ▪ Ellen Goodman, *Girls Will Be Girls, Unfortunately*

Unparalleled pedagogy and visuals

Reflected in the Database's themes

Fourteen thematic categories are included in **The Sundance Choice Database** to help students identify with the readings. The latest issues are examined within the following themes:

- American Identity: Melting Pot or Mosaic?
- The War on Terrorism
- Medical Malpractice
- Reparations for Slavery
- Fatherhood
- Abortion: Roe vs. Wade at Thirty
- Islam and the West

- Capital Punishment
- Immigration
- Global Warming
- Public Schools
- America's Role in the Twenty-First Century
- Gender Identity: Raising Boys and Girls
- Welfare to Work

Medical Malpractice

The health and life of my patients will be my first consideration.
−The Hippocratic Oath

The problem with medical malpractice is that it occurs far too often. It is the eighth leading cause of death in America, killing more people than AIDS, breast cancer, or automobile crashes.
−Leo Boyle

The villain, I believe, is our legal system, which has become a free-for-all, lacking the reliability and consistency that are essential to everyone, especially doctors and patients. Most victims of error get nothing, while others win lottery-like jury awards even when the doctor did nothing wrong.
−Philip K. Howard

I am sure I could have become a millionaire by suing my father's doctors and the hospital.... But I didn't.... [T]o sue someone for failing to be the god we wanted strikes me as wrong.
−Alden Blodget

OMFORT ALWAYS"

icians in the United States had only a fragmen-
icine. Few medical schools were affiliated with
not even accredited. Some medical schools did
ve a high school diploma. In a few states it was
al license in six months. Apprenticed to older
earned primarily by observation. There were
es, and little connection was made between
pped with dubious medicines and crude surgical
equently able to provide little more than emo-
eat many conditions, physicians attempted only

The War on Terrorism

How can you defeat an enemy who thinks he's on a mission from God? How? A hundred days and one war later, we know the answer: B-52's, for starters.
−Charles Krauthammer

The instinct to retaliate with bombing is an anachronism. Fewer than twenty men had brought us to our national knees.... The government's answer was that we were good and love freedom and these people are bad and hate it. That vapid answer came from a national culture that has lost its talent for healthy guilt.
−Daniel C. Maguire

[W]e hit Saddam for one simple reason: because we could, and because he deserved it and because he was right in the heart of that world. And don't believe the nonsense that this has had no effect. Every neighboring government—and 98 percent of terrorism is about what governments let happen—got the message. If you talk to U.S. soldiers in Iraq they will tell you this is what the war was about.
−Thomas L. Friedman

Real wars are not metaphors. And real wars have a beginning and an end.... But the war that has been decreed by the Bush administration will never end. That is one sign that it is not a war, but, rather, a mandate for expanding the use of American power.
−Susan Sontag

On the morning of September 11, 2001, President Bush was visiting a school. Informed that two planes had just crashed into the World Trade Center, Andrew Card, the White House Chief of Staff, interrupted the ceremony and whispered to the President, "America is under attack."
But was America at war?

Complete with customized technology integration

No other publisher offers a custom database of this quality with technology integrated into each customized reader. When you adopt **The Sundance Choice Database,** you have the option of choosing from a menu of interactive technology tools—each of which will be carefully integrated into your customized reader.

 Companion Website
See **http://sundance.wadsworth.com** for information on writing process papers.

 E Reading: InfoTrac College Edition
http://www.infotrac-college.com

For Further Reading
E–Readings Online

Search for articles by author or title in InfoTrac College Edition after entering your user name and password.

Barbara Hemphill, *Who Are You?*
Specific steps can protect consumers against identity theft.

Lance Davis, *Cities Use Environmental Design to Combat Crime.*
Cities use three principles in designing public buildings to deter crime.

San Fernando Valley Business Journal, *The Interview Process—How to Select the "Right" Person*
Employers can improve their ability to locate and hire the best applicants by improving their interview techniques.

Mark Moring, *This is Not Your High School English Class*
Moring explains how improved time management and study skills can help college students cope.

Louise S. Durham, *Climate of Controversy: The Causes of Global Warming Are Still a Matter of Debate, but It's Worth Understanding How the Process Works*

Two interactive and easy-to-use technology tools that are FREE with your adoption and can be integrated in your own reader are:

■ **Comp21: Composition in the 21st Century:** The first CD-ROM designed to help students navigate today's new writing contexts and to incorporate new sources. The CD-ROM includes visual libraries, audio and video galleries, and collections of classic essays and speeches to add texture and depth to student projects. The CD-ROM is linked to each theme or mode in the **Database.**

■ **InfoTrac College Edition with InfoMarks™.** Each theme or mode in the Database ends with a list of further readings on **InfoTrac College Edition with InfoMarks™,** a fully searchable database offering more than 20 years worth of full-text articles. *See page 6 for a complete description of* **InfoTrac College Edition.**

Clearly integrated technology

Reliable, cutting-edge web resources

That make research easy for students

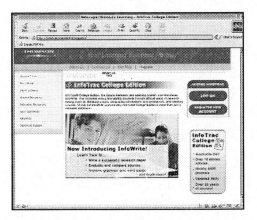

InfoTrac® College Edition with InfoMarks™

NOT SOLD SEPARATELY. This fully searchable database offers more than 20 years' worth of full-text articles (not abstracts) from almost 5,000 diverse sources, such as top academic journals, newsletters, and up-to-the-minute periodicals including *Time, Newsweek, Science, Forbes,* and *USA Today.* **NEW!** Your 4-month free subscription now includes instant access to virtual readers drawing from the vast **InfoTrac College Edition** library and hand-selected to work with your book. In addition, students have instant access to *InfoWrite,* which includes guides to writing research papers, grammar, "critical thinking" guidelines, and much more. Adopters and their students receive FREE unlimited access to **InfoTrac College Edition with InfoMarks** for four months. To take a quick tour of InfoTrac, visit **http://www.infotrac-college.com** and select the "User Demo." *(Journals subject to change. Certain restrictions may apply. For additional information, please consult your local Thomson representative.)*

Opposing Viewpoints Resource Center

0-534-12853-X

NOT SOLD SEPARATELY. This online center helps you expose your students to all sides of today's most compelling social and scientific issues, from genetic engineering to environmental policy, prejudice, abortion, health care reform, violence in the media, and much more. **The Opposing Viewpoints Resource Center** draws on Greenhaven Press's acclaimed social issues series, popular periodicals and newspapers, and core reference content from other Gale and Macmillan Reference USA sources. The result is a dynamic online library of current events topics—the facts as well as the arguments as articulated by the proponents and detractors of each position. Visit **http://www.gale.com/OpposingViewpoints.** *For college and university adopters only.*

Online resources

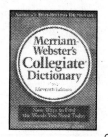

Table of Contents

WILLIAM F. BUCKLEY, JR.

For more than half a century, William F. Buckley, Jr. (1925–) has been one of America's most visible and prolific political commentators. As an essayist, newspaper columnist, founding editor of National Review *magazine, and long-time host of television's* Firing Line, *Buckley has probably done more than any other individual to make conservatism an intellectually respectable political philosophy. He is also a prolific novelist and the author of many occasional and familiar essays that have nothing to do with partisan politics. In 1965, he ran unsuccessfully for mayor of New York City on the Conservative Party ticket.*

Why Don't We Complain?

CONTEXT: *In "Why Don't We Complain?," which appeared in his first collection of essays,* Rumbles Left and Right *(1963), Buckley takes Americans to task for their willingness to put up with the avoidable annoyances of everyday life. Although his tone is light and humorous and his argument apolitical, Buckley projects the persona of a man who is unafraid to speak out when he is convinced that he is right. This is essentially the image he has fostered throughout his public career.*

1   It was the very last coach and the only empty seat on the entire train, so there was no turning back. The problem was to breathe. Outside, the temperature was below freezing. Inside the railroad car the temperature must have been about 85 degrees. I took off my overcoat, and a few minutes later my jacket, and noticed that the car was flecked with the white shirts of the passengers. I soon found my hand moving to loosen my tie. From one end of the car to the other, as we rattled through Westchester County, we sweated; but we did not moan.

2   I watched the train conductor appear at the head of the car. "Tickets, all tickets, please!" In a more virile age, I thought, the passengers would seize the conductor and strap him down on a seat over the radiator to share the fate of his patrons. He shuffled down the aisle, picking up tickets, punching commutation cards. *No one addressed a word to him.* He approached my seat, and I drew a deep breath of resolution. "Conductor," I began with a considerable edge to my voice. Instantly the doleful eyes of my seatmate turned tiredly from his newspaper to fix me with a resentful stare: What question could be so important as to justify my sibilant intrusion into his stupor? I was shaken by those eyes. I am incapable of making

a discreet fuss, so I mumbled a question about what time we were due in Stamford (I didn't even ask whether it would be before or after dehydration could be expected to set in), got my reply, and went back to my newspaper and to wiping my brow.

3   The conductor had nonchalantly walked down the gauntlet of eighty sweating American freemen, and not one of them had asked him to explain why the passengers in that car had been consigned to suffer. There is nothing to be done when the temperature *outdoors* is 85 degrees, and indoors the air conditioner has broken down; obviously when that happens there is nothing to do, except perhaps curse the day that one was born. But when the temperature outdoors is below freezing, it takes a positive act of will on somebody's part to set the temperature *indoors* at 85. Somewhere a valve was turned too far, a furnace overstocked, a thermostat maladjusted: something that could easily be remedied by turning off the heat and allowing the great outdoors to come indoors. All this is so obvious. What is not obvious is what has happened to the American people.

4   It isn't just the commuters, whom we have come to visualize as a supine breed who have got on to the trick of suspending their sensory faculties twice a day while they submit to the creeping dissolution of the railroad industry. It isn't just they who have given up trying to rectify irrational vexations. It is the American people everywhere.

5   A few weeks ago at a large movie theater I turned to my wife and said, "The picture is out of focus." "Be quiet," she answered. I obeyed. But a few minutes later I raised the point again, with mounting impatience. "It will be all right in a minute," she said apprehensively. (She would rather lose her eyesight than be around when I make one of my infrequent scenes.) I waited. It was *just* out of focus—not glaringly out, but out. My vision is 20-20, and I assume that is the vision, adjusted, for most people in the movie house. So, after hectoring my wife throughout the first reel, I finally prevailed upon her to admit that it *was* off, and very annoying. We then settled down, coming to rest on the presumption that: a) someone connected with the management of the theater must soon notice the blur and make the correction; or b) that someone seated near the rear of the house would make the complaint in behalf of those of us up front; or c) that—any minute now—the entire house would explode into catcalls and foot stamping, calling dramatic attention to the irksome distortion.

6   What happened was nothing. The movie ended, as it had begun, *just* out of focus, and as we trooped out, we stretched our faces in a variety of contortions to accustom the eye to the shock of normal focus.

7   I think it is safe to say that everybody suffered on that occasion. And I think it is safe to assume that everyone was expecting someone else to take

the initiative in going back to speak to the manager. And it is probably true even that if we had supposed the movie would run right through the blurred image, someone surely would have summoned up the purposive indignation to get up out of his seat and file his complaint.

8   But notice that no one did. And the reason no one did is because we are all increasingly anxious in America to be unobtrusive, we are reluctant to make our voices heard, hesitant about claiming our rights; we are afraid that our cause is unjust, or that if it is not unjust, that it is ambiguous; or if not even that, that it is too trivial to justify the horrors of a confrontation with Authority; we will sit in an oven or endure a racking headache before undertaking a head-on, I'm-here-to-tell-you complaint. That tendency to passive compliance, to a heedless endurance, is something to keep one's eyes on—in sharp focus.

9   I myself can occasionally summon the courage to complain, but I cannot, as I have intimated, complain softly. My own instinct is so strong to let the thing ride, to forget about it—to expect that someone will take the matter up, when the grievance is collective, in my behalf—that it is only when the provocation is at a very special key, whose vibrations touch simultaneously a complexus of nerves, allergies, and passions, that I catch fire and find the reserves of courage and assertiveness to speak up. When that happens, I get quite carried away. My blood gets hot, my brow wet, I become unbearably and unconscionably sarcastic and bellicose; I am girded for a total showdown.

10   Why should that be? Why could not I (or anyone else) on that railroad coach have said simply to the conductor, "Sir"—I take that back: that sounds sarcastic—"Conductor, would you be good enough to turn down the heat? I am extremely hot. In fact, I tend to get hot every time the temperature reaches 85 degr—." Strike that last sentence. Just end it with the simple statement that you are extremely hot, and let the conductor infer the cause.

11   Every New Year's Eve I resolve to do something about the Milquetoast in me and vow to speak up, calmly, for my rights, and for the betterment of our society, on every appropriate occasion. Entering last New Year's Eve I was fortified in my resolve because that morning at breakfast I had had to ask the waitress three times for a glass of milk. She finally brought it—after I had finished my eggs, which is when I don't want it anymore. I did not have the manliness to order her to take the milk back, but settled instead for a cowardly sulk, and ostentatiously refused to drink the milk—though I later paid for it—rather than state plainly to the hostess, as I should have, why I had not drunk it, and would not pay for it.

12   So by the time the New Year ushered out the Old, riding in on my morning's indignation and stimulated by the gastric juices of resolution that flow so faithfully on New Year's Eve, I rendered my vow. Henceforward I would

conquer my shyness, my despicable disposition to supineness. I would speak out like a man against the unnecessary annoyances of our time.

13   Forty-eight hours later, I was standing in line at the ski repair store in Pico Peak, Vermont. All I needed, to get on with my skiing, was the loan, for one minute, of a small screwdriver, to tighten a loose binding. Behind the counter in the workshop were two men. One was industriously engaged in servicing the complicated requirements of a young lady at the head of the line, and obviously he would be tied up for quite a while. The other— "Jiggs," his workmate called him—was a middle-aged man, who sat in a chair puffing a pipe, exchanging small talk with his working partner. My pulse began its tell-tale acceleration. The minutes ticked on. I stared at the idle shopkeeper, hoping to shame him into action, but he was impervious to my telepathic reproof and continued his small talk with his friend, brazenly insensitive to the nervous demands of six good men who were raring to ski.

14   Suddenly my New Year's Eve resolution struck me. It was now or never. I broke from my place in line and marched to the counter. I was going to control myself. I dug my nails into my palms. My effort was only partially successful.

15   "If you are not too busy," I said icily, "would you mind handing me a screwdriver?"

16   Work stopped and everyone turned his eyes on me, and I experienced that mortification I always feel when I am the center of centripetal shafts of curiosity, resentment, perplexity.

17   But the worst was yet to come. "I am sorry, sir," said Jiggs deferentially, moving the pipe from his mouth. "I am not supposed to move. I have just had a heart attack." That was the signal for a great whirring noise that descended from heaven. We looked, stricken, out the window, and it appeared as though a cyclone had suddenly focused on the snowy courtyard between the shop and the ski lift. Suddenly a gigantic army helicopter materialized, and hovered down to a landing. Two men jumped out of the plane carrying a stretcher, tore into the ski shop, and lifted the shopkeeper onto the stretcher. Jiggs bade his companion good-bye and was whisked out the door, into the plane, up to the heavens, down—we learned—to a nearby army hospital. I looked up manfully—into a score of man eating eyes. I put the experience down as a reversal.

18   As I write this, on an airplane, I have run out of paper and need to reach into my briefcase under my legs for more. I cannot do this until my empty lunch tray is removed from my lap. I arrested the stewardess as she passed empty-handed down the aisle on the way to the kitchen to fetch the lunch trays for the passengers up forward who haven't been served yet. "Would

you please take my tray?" "Just a *moment*, sir!" she said, and marched on sternly. Shall I tell her that since she is headed for the kitchen anyway, it could not delay the feeding of the other passengers by more than two seconds necessary to stash away my empty tray? Or remind her that not fifteen minutes ago she spoke unctuously into the loudspeaker the words undoubtedly devised by the airline's highly paid public relations counselor: "If there is anything I or Miss French can do for you to make your trip more enjoyable, *please* let us—" I have run out of paper.

19   I think the observable reluctance of the majority of Americans to assert themselves in minor matters is related to our increased sense of helplessness in an age of technology and centralized political and economic power. For generations, Americans who were too hot, or too cold, got up and did something about it. Now we call the plumber, or the electrician, or the furnace man. The habit of looking after our own needs obviously had something to do with the assertiveness that characterized the American family familiar to readers of American literature. With the technification of life goes our direct responsibility for our material environment, and we are conditioned to adopt a position of helplessness not only as regards the broken air conditioner, but as regards the overheated train. It takes an expert to fix the former, but not the latter; yet these distinctions, as we withdraw into helplessness, tend to fade away.

20   Our notorious political apathy is a related phenomenon. Every year, whether the Republican or the Democratic Party is in office, more and more power drains away from the individual to feed vast reservoirs in far-off places; and we have less and less say about the shape of events which shape our future. From this alienation of personal power comes the sense of resignation with which we accept the political dispensations of a powerful government whose hold upon us continues to increase.

21   An editor of a national weekly news magazine told me a few years ago that as few as a dozen letters of protest against an editorial stance of his magazine was enough to convene a plenipotentiary meeting of the board of editors to review policy. "So few people complain, or make their voices heard," he explained to me, "that we assume a dozen letters represent the inarticulated views of thousands of readers." In the past ten years, he said, the volume of mail has noticeably decreased, even though the circulation of his magazine has risen.

22   When our voices are finally mute, when we have finally suppressed the natural instinct to complain, whether the vexation is trivial or grave, we shall have become automatons, incapable of feeling. When Premier Khrushchev first came to this country late in 1959 he was primed, we are

informed, to experience the bitter resentment of the American people against his tyranny, against his persecutions, against the movement which is responsible for the great number of American deaths in Korea, for billions in taxes every year, and for life everlasting on the brink of disaster; but Khrushchev was pleasantly surprised, and reported back to the Russian people that he had been met with overwhelming cordiality (read: apathy), except, to be sure, for "a few fascists who followed me around with their wretched posters, and should be horsewhipped."

23   I may be crazy, but I say there would have been lots more posters in a society where train temperatures in the dead of winter are not allowed to climb to 85 degrees without complaint.

Understanding Meaning

1. Is Buckley's purpose in the essay merely to complain about what he sees as Americans' unwillingness to speak up, or is there something he wants Americans to do to solve what he perceives to be a problem?
2. What examples does he provide of people's tendency not to complain?
3. What happened in the one example when he did complain?
4. What does Buckley speculate might be the reason that we are hesitant to complain? What does this hesitancy have to do with technology and politics?
5. *CRITICAL THINKING.* When you fail to complain in situations such as the ones that Buckley describes, is it for the reasons that Buckley suggests? Are there other reasons why you are sometimes hesitant to speak up? Explain.

Evaluating Strategy

1. How effective are Buckley's examples in proving the point that he is trying to make? Do you feel that he could have made a strong case without using examples?
2. *BLENDING THE MODES.* Why is starting a piece with a narrative sometimes a good tactic even if narrative is not the primary mode of the piece?
3. What difference does it make that Buckley chose to use first person in this piece?

Appreciating Language

1. Buckley uses quite a few words that may not be a normal part of your conversation: *supine, sibilant,* and *unctuously,* for example. Did you find his vocabulary interfering with your ability to understand his ideas? Why or why not?

2. If you are familiar with William F. Buckley, explain how the tone and diction in the piece seem appropriate for him. If not, what mental image of the writer comes to your mind as you read? What age? Wearing what sort of clothes? What else?

3. Buckley obviously feels strongly about this subject. Does his writing come across as emotional, reasonable, or both? Explain.

Writing Suggestions

1. *COLLABORATIVE WRITING.* Brainstorm with your group, listing those times you have seen people act as Buckley describes, keeping their complaints to themselves rather than expressing them. Also think about times when one person did speak up.

2. Use your discussion from Writing Suggestion #1 above as the starting point for an essay in which you provide examples from your experience that support Buckley's claim or that illustrate that there is the occasional individual who does not hesitate to complain.

3. Use Buckley's essay as a model to write an essay about a form of behavior that annoys you in a way similar to the way that people's failure to complain annoys him. Use examples to build your case.

ANNIE DILLARD

Annie Dillard (1945–) was born in Pittsburg, Pennsylvania, and received her BA and MA degrees from Hollins College in Virginia in the 1960s. Her first book, Pilgrim at Tinker Creek *(1974), won the Pulitzer Prize for general nonfiction. She has published twelve subsequent books, including collections of poetry, a historical novel, and several volumes of essays. In 1999, she was inducted into the American Academy of Arts and Letters.*

The Chase

CONTEXT: *The following selection comes from Dillard's autobiographical narrative An American Childhood (1987). Born in 1945, she was part of the largest generation of children in American history. The incident recorded here occurred in December 1952, when she was seven. Looking back on it from her perspective as an adult, she captures the brash self-assurance of childhood that still existed in her adult "victim."*

1   Some boys taught me to play football. This was fine sport. You thought up a new strategy for every play and whispered it to the others. You went out for a pass, fooling everyone. Best, you got to throw yourself mightily at someone's running legs. Either you brought him down or you hit the ground flat on your chin, with your arms empty before you. It was all or nothing. If you hesitated in fear, you would miss and get hurt: you would take a hard fall while the kid got away, or you would get kicked in the face while the kid got away. But if you flung yourself wholeheartedly at the back of his knees—if you gathered and joined body and soul and pointed them diving fearlessly—then you likely wouldn't get hurt, and you'd stop the ball. Your fate, and your team's score, depended on your concentration and courage. Nothing girls did could compare with it.

2   Boys welcomed me at baseball, too, for I had, through enthusiastic practice, what was weirdly known as a boy's arm. In winter, in the snow, there was neither baseball nor football, so the boys and I threw snowballs at passing cars. I got in trouble throwing snowballs, and have seldom been happier since.

3   On one weekday morning after Christmas, six inches of new snow had just fallen. We were standing up to our boot tops in snow on a front yard on trafficked Reynolds Street, waiting for cars. The cars traveled Reynolds

Street slowly and evenly; they were targets all but wrapped in red ribbons, cream puffs. We couldn't miss.

4   I was seven; the boys were eight, nine, and ten. The oldest two Fahey boys were there—Mikey and Peter—polite blond boys who lived near me on Lloyd Street, and who already had four brothers and sisters. My parents approved Mikey and Peter Fahey. Chickie McBride was there, a tough kid, and Billy Paul and Mackie Kean too, from across Reynolds, where the boys grew up dark and furious, grew up skinny, knowing, and skilled. We had all drifted from our houses that morning looking for action, and had found it here on Reynolds Street.

5   It was cloudy but cold. The cars' tires laid behind them on the snowy street a complex trail of beige chunks like crenellated castle walls. I had stepped on some earlier; they squeaked. We could have wished for more traffic. When a car came, we all popped it one. In the intervals between cars we reverted to the natural solitude of children.

6   I started making an iceball—a perfect iceball, from perfectly white snow, perfectly spherical, and squeezed perfectly translucent so no snow remained all the way through. (The Fahey boys and I considered it unfair actually to throw an iceball at somebody, but it had been known to happen.)

7   I had just embarked on the iceball project when we heard tire chains come clanking from afar. A black Buick was moving toward us down the street. We all spread out, banged together some regular snowballs, took aim, and, when the Buick drew nigh, fired.

8   A soft snowball hit the driver's windshield right before the driver's face. It made a smashed star with a hump in the middle.

9   Often, of course, we hit our target, but this time, the only time in all of life, the car pulled over and stopped. Its wide black door opened; a man got out of it, running. He didn't even close the car door.

10   He ran after us, and we ran away from him, up the snowy Reynolds sidewalk. At the corner, I looked back; incredibly, he was still after us. He was in city clothes: a suit and tie, street shoes. Any normal adult would have quit, having sprung us into flight and made his point. This man was gaining on us. He was a thin man, all action. All of a sudden, we were running for our lives.

11   Wordless, we split up. We were on our turf; we could lose ourselves in the neighborhood backyards, everyone for himself. I paused and considered. Everyone had vanished except Mikey Fahey, who was just rounding the corner of a yellow brick house. Poor Mikey, I trailed him. The driver of the Buick sensibly picked the two of us to follow. The man apparently had all day.

12   He chased Mikey and me around the yellow house and up a backyard path we knew by heart: under a low tree, up a bank, through a hedge, down some snowy steps, and across the grocery store's delivery driveway. We smashed through a gap in another hedge, entered a scruffy backyard and ran around its back porch and tight between houses to Edgerton Avenue; we ran across Edgerton to an alley and up our own sliding woodpile to the Halls' front yard; he kept coming. We ran up Lloyd Street and wound through mazy backyards toward the steep hilltop at Willard and Lang.

13   He chased us silently, block after block. He chased us silently over picket fences, through thorny hedges, between houses, around garbage cans, and across streets. Every time I glanced back, choking for breath, I expected he would have quit. He must have been as breathless as we were. His jacket strained over his body. It was an immense discovery, pounding into my hot head with every sliding, joyous step, that this ordinary adult evidently knew what I thought only children who trained at football knew: that you have to fling yourself at what you're doing, you have to point yourself, forget yourself, aim, dive.

14   Mikey and I had nowhere to go, in our own neighborhood or out of it, but away from this man who was chasing us. He impelled us forward; we compelled him to follow our route. The air was cold; every breath tore my throat. We kept running, block after block; we kept improvising, backyard after backyard, running, a frantic course and choosing it simultaneously, failing always to find small places or hard places to slow him down, and discovering always, exhilarated, dismayed, that only bare speed could save us—for he would never give up, this man—and we were losing speed.

15   He chased us through the backyard labyrinths of ten blocks before he caught us by our jackets. He caught us and we all stopped.

16   We three stood staggering, half blinded, coughing, in an obscure hilltop backyard: a man in his twenties, a boy, a girl. He had released our jackets, our pursuer, our captor, our hero: He knew we weren't going anywhere. We all played by the rules. Mikey and I unzipped our jackets. I pulled off my sopping mittens. Our tracks multiplied in the backyard's new snow. We had been breaking new snow all morning. We didn't look at each other. I was cherishing my excitement. The man's lower pants legs were wet; his cuffs were full of snow, and there was a prow of snow beneath them on his shoes and socks. Some trees bordered the little flat backyard, some messy winter trees. There was no one around: a clearing in a grove, and we the only players.

17   It was a long time before he could speak. I had some difficulty at first recalling why we were there. My lips felt swollen; I couldn't see out of the sides of my eyes; I kept coughing.

18   "You stupid kids," he began perfunctorily.

19   We listened perfunctorily indeed, if we listened at all, for the chewing out was redundant, a mere formality, and beside the point. The point was that he had chased us passionately without giving up, and so he had caught us. Now he came down to earth. I wanted the glory to last forever.

20   But how could the glory have lasted forever? We could have run through every backyard in North America until we got to Panama. But when he trapped us at the lip of the Panama Canal, what precisely could he have done to prolong the drama of the chase and cap its glory? I brooded about this for the next few years. He could only have fried Mikey Fahey and me in boiling oil, say, or dismembered us piecemeal, or staked us to anthills. None of which I really wanted, and none of which any adult was likely to do, even in the spirit of fun. He could only chew us out there in the Panamanian jungle, after months or years of exalting pursuit. He could only begin, "You stupid kids," and continue in his ordinary Pittsburgh accent with his normal righteous anger and the usual common sense.

21   If in that snowy backyard the driver of the black Buick had cut off our heads, Mikey's and mine, I would have died happy, for nothing has required so much of me since as being chased all over Pittsburgh in the middle of winter—running terrified, exhausted—by this sainted, skinny, furious red-headed man who wished to have a word with us. I don't know how he found his way back to his car.

Understanding Meaning

1.   Dillard draws her readers into the chase through her snow-covered neighborhood in Pittsburg, but she also does a masterful job of explaining how this run of her life made her feel. Which sentence or two best sum up her thesis in the essay?

2.   Dillard opens the essay with a discussion of her love of sports, as opposed to more traditional girls' activities. She goes further to explain how football should be played to get the most satisfaction out of it. How does that explanation relate to the chase she then narrates?

3.   What does the driver do when he catches the two children? Why is that not as important, finally, as the chase itself?

4.   Even when it comes to throwing snowballs at passing cars, there are rules that must be followed. What are some of those rules? Does Dillard play by the rules?

5.   *CRITICAL THINKING.* Have you ever been involved in a sport in which having fun was really more important than winning? Explain.

Evaluating Strategy

1. Part of the purpose of Dillard's opening paragraph is to establish her love
    of sports. It also, however, establishes her opinion about how to get the
    most out of a sport. How does one do that? Why is it important to the suc-
    cess of Dillard's narrative that she establish that in the beginning?
2. Once the chase begins, Dillard must report the facts of the chase accu-
    rately while also capturing her feelings about what is happening. Her use
    of first-person narration is a natural choice for doing that. Where, specifi-
    cally, does she let us know how she feels about the chase?
3. Where does Dillard link the chase to the reference to football that opened
    the essay?
4. *CRITICAL THINKING.* There is virtually no dialogue in this essay. What
    are some of the practical reasons there is little dialogue? Why is little dia-
    logue necessary?

Appreciating Language

1. At times Dillard juxtaposes opposites to show the delight and the fear that
    she experiences at the same time as she runs. One example is when she
    says in paragraph 14 that she was both *exhilarated* and *dismayed* that the
    man was gaining on them. Where else do you find such pairings?
2. What does Dillard mean when she describes the cars on Reynolds Street
    as "all but wrapped in red ribbons, cream puffs"?

Writing Suggestions

1. Recall a time when you knew that something you were doing was danger-
    ous but did it anyway because of the thrill, the excitement, the rush of
    adrenaline. Use Dillard's essay as a model to write an essay in which you
    capture the mixture of emotions you felt.
2. *COLLABORATIVE WRITING.* Exchange drafts with a member of your
    group. See if your reader can pick out your thesis statement or, if there is
    no single sentence that sums up your thesis, can write in a single sentence
    what the thesis seems to be. Discuss where each author placed the thesis
    and whether that placement is best or, if the thesis is implied, whether that
    is the best choice.
3. Rewrite Dillard's narrative from the point of view of the driver who chased
    them.

JAMES DILLARD

James Dillard is a physician who specializes in rehabilitation medicine. In this narrative, first published in the "My Turn" column in Newsweek, *he relates an incident that nearly ended his medical career.*

A Doctor's Dilemma

CONTEXT: *As you read this narrative, keep in mind how most people expect physicians to respond in a life-threatening emergency.*

1   It was a bright, clear February afternoon in Gettysburg. A strong sun and layers of down did little to ease the biting cold. Our climb to the crest of Little Roundtop wound past somber monuments, barren trees and polished cannon. From the top, we peered down on the wheat field where men had fallen so close together that one could not see the ground. Rifle balls had whined as thick as bee swarms through the trees, and cannon shots had torn limbs from the young men fighting there. A frozen wind whipped tears from your eyes. My friend Amy huddled close, using me as a wind breaker. Despite the cold, it was hard to leave this place.

2   Driving east out of Gettysburg on a country blacktop, the gray Bronco ahead of us passed through a rural crossroad just as a small pickup truck tried to take a left turn. The Bronco swerved, but slammed into the pickup on the passenger's side. We immediately slowed to a crawl as we passed the scene. The Bronco's driver looked fine, but we couldn't see the driver of the pickup. I pulled over on the shoulder and got out to investigate.

3   The right side of the truck was smashed in, and the side window was shattered. The driver was partly out of the truck. His head hung forward over the edge of the passenger-side window, the front of his neck crushed on the shattered windowsill. He was unconscious and starting to turn a dusky blue. His chest slowly heaved against a blocked windpipe.

4   A young man ran out of a house at the crossroad. "Get an ambulance out here," I shouted against the wind. "Tell them a man is dying."

5   I looked down again at the driver hanging from the windowsill. There were six empty beer bottles on the floor of the truck. I could smell the beer through the window. I knew I had to move him, to open his airway. I had no

idea what neck injuries he had sustained. He could easily end up a quadri-plegic. But I thought: he'll be dead by the time the ambulance gets here if I don't move him and try to do something to help him.

6   An image flashed before my mind. I could see the courtroom and the driver of the truck sitting in a wheelchair. I could see his attorney pointing at me and thundering at the jury: "This young doctor, with still a year left in his residency training, took it upon himself to play God. He took it upon himself to move this gravely injured man, condemning him forever to this wheelchair . . ." I imagined the millions of dollars in award money. And all the years of hard work lost. I'd be paying him off for the rest of my life. Amy touched my shoulder. "What are you going to do?"

7   The automatic response from long hours in the emergency room kicked in. I pulled off my overcoat and rolled up my sleeves. The trick would be to keep enough traction straight up on his head while I moved his torso, so that his probable broken neck and spinal-cord injury wouldn't be made worse. Amy came around the driver's side, climbed half in and grabbed his belt and shirt collar. Together we lifted him off the windowsill.

8   He was still out cold, limp as a rag doll. His throat was crushed and blood from the jugular vein was running down my arms. He still couldn't breathe. He was deep blue-magenta now, his pulse was rapid and thready. The stench of alcohol turned my stomach, but I positioned his jaw and tried to blow air down into his lungs. It wouldn't go.

9   Amy had brought some supplies from my car. I opened an oversize intravenous needle and groped on the man's neck. My hands were numb, covered with freezing blood and bits of broken glass. Hyoid bone—God, I can't even feel the thyroid cartilage, it's gone . . . OK, the thyroid gland is about there, cricoid rings are here . . . we'll go in right here . . .

10   It was a lucky first shot. Pink air sprayed through the IV needle. I placed a second needle next to the first. The air began whistling through it. Almost immediately, the driver's face turned bright red. After a minute, his pulse slowed down and his eyes moved slightly. I stood up, took a step back and looked down. He was going to make it. He was going to live. A siren wailed in the distance. I turned and saw Amy holding my overcoat. I was shivering and my arms were turning white with cold.

11   The ambulance captain looked around and bellowed, "What the hell . . . who did this?" as his team scurried over to the man lying in the truck.

12   "I did," I replied. He took down my name and address for his reports. I had just destroyed my career. I would never be able to finish my residency with a massive lawsuit pending. My life was over.

13   The truck driver was strapped onto a backboard, his neck in a stiff collar. The ambulance crew had controlled the bleeding and started intravenous fluid. He was slowly waking up. As they loaded him into the ambulance, I saw him move his feet. Maybe my future wasn't lost.

14   A police sergeant called me from Pennsylvania three weeks later. Six days after successful throat-reconstruction surgery, the driver had signed out, against medical advice, from the hospital because he couldn't get a drink on the ward. He was being arraigned on drunk-driving charges.

15   A few days later, I went into the office of one of my senior professors, to tell the story. He peered over his half glasses and his eyes narrowed. "Well, you did the right thing medically of course. But, James, do you know what you put at risk by doing that?" he said sternly. "What was I supposed to do?" I asked.

16   "Drive on," he replied. "There is an army of lawyers out there who would stand in line to get a case like that. If that driver had turned out to be a quadriplegic, you might never have practiced medicine again. You were a very lucky young man."

17   The day I graduated from medical school, I took an oath to serve the sick and the injured. I remember truly believing I would be able to do just that. But I have found out it isn't so simple. I understand now what a foolish thing I did that day. Despite my oath, I know what I would do on that cold roadside near Gettysburg today. I would drive on.

Understanding Meaning

1. What was Dillard's goal in publishing this narrative in a national news magazine?

2. Does this narrative serve to contrast ideals and reality? How does Dillard's oath conflict with his final decision?

3. Does the fact that the victim had been drinking alcohol have an impact on your reactions to the doctor's actions? Does it seem to affect Dillard's feeling toward the man?

4. *CRITICAL THINKING.* Do medical malpractice suits improve or diminish the quality of medicine? Are lawyers or eager-to-sue patients to blame for the author's decision to "drive on" next time?

Evaluating Strategy

1. *BLENDING THE MODES.* Does this narrative also serve as a persuasive argument? Is this story a better vehicle than a standard argumentative essay that states a thesis and presents factual support?
2. Does this first-person story help place the reader in the doctor's position? Is this a more effective strategy than writing an objective third-person essay about the impact of malpractice suits?
3. Why does Dillard mention that the patient later disobeyed his doctor's orders and left the hospital so he could get a drink?
4. How do you think Dillard wanted his readers to respond to the essay's last line?

Appreciating Language

1. What words does Dillard use to dramatize his attempts to save the driver's life? How do they reflect the tension he felt?
2. What language does Dillard use to demonstrate what he was risking by trying to save a life?
3. What kind of people read *Newsweek*? Do you find this essay's language suitable?

Writing Suggestions

1. Relate an emergency situation you have experienced or encountered. Using Dillard's essay as a model, write an account capturing what you thought and felt as you acted.
2. Write a letter to the editor of *Newsweek* in response to Dillard's essay. Do you find Dillard's position tenable? Are you angry at a doctor who vows not to help strangers in daily life? Or do you blame the legal community for putting a physician in this position?
3. *COLLABORATIVE WRITING.* Discuss Dillard's essay with a number of students and list their reactions. Write a division paper outlining their views.

GRETEL EHRLICH

Although she was born in Santa Barbara, California, Gretel Ehrlich (1946–) has long made her home in Wyoming. Her books include a collection of short fiction called Drinking Dry Clouds: Stories from Wyoming *(1991), a novel called* Heart Mountain *(1988) and two volumes of poetry. Her magazine articles and essays have been collected in* The Solace of Open Spaces *(1985) and* Islands, the Universe, Home *(1991).*

About Men

CONTEXT: *Although the following essay from* The Solace of Open Spaces *is called "About Men," it deals specifically with the definition of manhood embodied by the western cowboy. From the dime novels of the late nineteenth century through the serialized films of the 1930s and '40s to the television dramas of the '50s and '60s, a particular image of the cowboy has become an enduring stereotype in American popular culture. In writing about the differences between the cowboy myth and the reality she has observed, Ehrlich gives us a more complex, nuanced, and positive view of the very concept of masculinity.*

1   When I'm in New York but feeling lonely for Wyoming. I look for the Marlboro ads in the subway. What I'm aching to see is horseflesh, the glint of a spur, a line of distant mountains, brimming creeks, and a reminder of the ranchers and cowboys I've ridden with for the last eight years. But the men I see in those posters with their stern, humorless looks remind me of no one I know here. In our hellbent earnestness to romanticize the cowboy we've ironically disesteemed his true character. If he's "strong and silent" it's because there's probably no one to talk to. If he "rides away into the sunset" it's because he's been on horseback since four in the morning moving cattle and he's trying, fifteen hours later, to get home to his family. If he's "a rugged individualist" he's also part of a team: Ranch work is teamwork and even the glorified open-range cowboys of the 1880s rode up and down the Chisholm Trail in the company of twenty or thirty other riders. Instead of the macho, trigger-happy man our culture has perversely wanted him to be, the cowboy is more apt to be convivial, quirky, and softhearted. To be "tough" on a ranch has nothing to do with conquests and displays of power. More often than not, circumstances—like the colt he's riding or an unexpected blizzard—are overpowering him. It's not toughness but "toughing it out" that counts. In other words, this macho cultural artifact the cowboy has

become is simply a man who possesses resilience, patience, and an instinct for survival. "Cowboys are just like a pile of rocks—everything happens to them. They get climbed on, kicked, rained and snowed on, scuffed up by wind. Their job is 'just to take it,'" one old-timer told me.

2   A cowboy is someone who loves his work. Since the hours are long—ten to fifteen hours a day—and the pay is $30 he has to. What's required of him is an odd mixture of physical vigor and maternalism. His part of the beef-raising industry is to birth and nurture calves and take care of their mothers. For the most part his work is done on horseback and in a lifetime he sees and comes to know more animals than people. The iconic myth surrounding him is built on American notions of heroism: the index of a man's value as measured in physical courage. Such ideas have perverted manliness into a self-absorbed race for cheap thrills. In a rancher's world, courage has less to do with facing danger than with acting spontaneously—usually on behalf of an animal or another rider. If a cow is stuck in a boghole he throws a loop around her neck, takes his dally (a half hitch around the saddle horn), and pulls her out with horsepower. If a calf is born sick, he may take her home, warm her in front of the kitchen fire, and massage her legs until dawn. One friend, whose favorite horse was trying to swim a lake with hobbles on, dove under water and cut her legs loose with a knife, then swam her to shore, his arm around her neck lifeguard-style, and saved her from drowning. Because these incidents are usually linked to someone or something outside himself, the westerner's courage is selfless, a form of compassion.

3   The physical punishment that goes with cowboying is greatly underplayed. Once fear is dispensed with, the threshold of pain rises to meet the demands of the job. When Jane Fonda asked Robert Redford (in the film *Electric Horseman*) if he was sick as he struggled to his feet one morning, he replied. "No, just bent." For once the movies had it right. The cowboys I was sitting with laughed in agreement. Cowboys are rarely complainers; they show their stoicism by laughing at themselves.

4   If a rancher or cowboy has been thought of as a "man's man"—laconic, hard-drinking, inscrutable—there's almost no place in which the balancing act between male and female, manliness and femininity, can be more natural. If he's gruff, handsome, and physically fit on the outside, he's androgynous at the core. Ranchers are midwives, hunters, nurturers, providers, and conservationists all at once. What we've interpreted as toughness—weathered skin, calloused hands, a squint in the eye and a growl in the voice—only masks the tenderness inside. "Now don't go telling me these lambs are cute," one rancher warned me the first day I walked into the football-field-sized

lambing sheds. The next thing I knew he was holding a black lamb. "Ain't this little rat good-lookin'?"

So many of the men who came to the West were southerners—men looking for work and a new life after the Civil War—that chivalrousness and strict codes of honor were soon thought of as western traits. There were very few women in Wyoming during territorial days, so when they did arrive (some as mail-order brides from places like Philadelphia) there was a stand-offishness between the sexes and a formality that persists now. Ranchers still tip their hats and say, "Howdy, ma'am" instead of shaking hands with me.

Even young cowboys are often evasive with women. It's not that they're Jekyll and Hyde creatures—gentle with animals and rough on women—but rather, that they don't know how to bring their tenderness into the house and lack the vocabulary to express the complexity of what they feel. Dancing wildly all night becomes a metaphor for the explosive emotions pent up inside, and when these are, on occasion, released, they're so battery-charged and potent that one caress of the face or one "I love you" will peal for a long while.

The geographical vastness and the social isolation here make emotional evolution seem impossible. Those contradictions of the heart between respectability, logic, and convention on the one hand, and impulse, passion, and intuition on the other, played out wordlessly against the paradisical beauty of the West, give cowboys a wide-eyed but drawn look. Their lips pucker up, not with kisses but with immutability. They may want to break out, staying up all night with a lover just to talk, but they don't know how and can't imagine what the consequences will be. Those rare occasions when they do bare themselves result in confusion. "I feel as if I'd sprained my heart," one friend told me a month after such a meeting.

My friend Ted Hoagland wrote, "No one is as fragile as a woman but no one is as fragile as a man." For all the women here who use "fragileness" to avoid work or as a sexual ploy, there are men who try to hide theirs, all the while clinging to an adolescent dependency on women to cook their meals, wash their clothes, and keep the ranch house warm in winter. But there is true vulnerability in evidence here. Because these men work with animals, not machines or numbers, because they live outside in landscapes of torrential beauty, because they are confined to a place and a routine embellished with awesome variables, because calves die in the arms that pulled others into life, because they go to the mountains as if on a pilgrimage to find out what makes a herd of elk tick, their strength is also a softness, their toughness, a rare delicacy.

Understanding Meaning

1. What does Ehrlich's purpose seem to have been in writing this essay?
2. According to paragraph 2, how is the cowboy's courage different from what she calls the "myth" of heroism? How does she use examples to illustrate a cowboy's compassionate courage?
3. What other characteristics of the cowboy does she exemplify?
4. In her second paragraph, Ehrlich says that cowboys are maternal. In paragraph 4, she says that they are androgynous. What point is she trying to make about cowboys by stressing characteristics that are usually associated with women?
5. How does Ehrlich say that cowboys relate to women? Why?
6. *CRITICAL THINKING.* Think about how cowboys are portrayed in movies that you have seen. Would the examples that come to mind fit into the image of the Marlboro Man that Ehrlich refers to? The image of the cowboy that Ehrlich presents? Neither? Explain.

Evaluating Strategy

1. Starting with the second paragraph, what general point is Ehrlich making about cowboys in each paragraph?
2. What are some of the examples that Ehrlich offers in support of each topic sentence?
3. Where does Ehrlich *stop* contrasting the reality of cowboy life with the "myth" that has grown up around it to focus only on the cowboy life?
4. Why is it a good tactic to use Marlboro ads as a way to introduce her essay?
5. What one or two sentences best summarize the main idea of Ehrlich's essay?

Appreciating Language

1. Ehrlich ends the first paragraph with a simile. What did the old-timer she is quoting compare cowboys to?
2. Several phrases in the first paragraph besides the ending quotation are in quotation marks. Why?
3. List some of the words and phrases that Ehrlich uses that are usually associated with women and some that are usually associated with men. How does Ehrlich use those terms to show that cowboys are a blend of the two?
4. Ehrlich refers to the "paradisical beauty" of the West (paragraph 7). In the last paragraph, she uses an even more unusual term: "torrential beauty." What ideas about nature is she trying to get across in using these particular terms?

Writing Suggestions

1. What image of the cowboy have you seen in movies and on television shows? Choose one characteristic of the screen cowboy and write an essay in which you give specific examples of movies, shows, characters, and/or actors who demonstrate that trait.

2. *COLLABORATIVE WRITING.* After reading what several of your class-mates wrote in response to Writing Suggestion #1 above, write a paragraph together in which you explain whether any of the examples used in their essays match Ehrlich's idea of the real cowboy.

3. Explain in an essay why it is necessary for a real cowboy to have both manly characteristics and maternal ones.

WILLIAM GOLDING

The British writer William Golding (1911–1993) is the author of such highly acclaimed novels as The Inheritors *(1955),* Pincher Martin *(1956),* Free Fall *(1959),* The Spire *(1964),* The Pyramid *(1967),* The Scorpion God *(1971),* Darkness Visible *(1975),* Rites of Passage *(1980), and* The Paper Men *(1984). He is best remembered, however, for his first novel,* The Lord of the Flies *(1954), a tale of human evil featuring a group of British schoolboys stranded on a desert island. Golding was awarded the Nobel Prize for Literature in 1983.*

Thinking as a Hobby

CONTEXT: *Golding purports to categorize types of thought as a pretext for categorizing types of people. Most persons (Grade 3) are too dimwitted to realize the inconsistencies between what they profess and how they act. Others (Grade 2) are bright enough to discern the inconsistencies of others but too superficial to think creatively themselves. The true genius (Grade 1) is so rare that the only example Golding can come up with is Albert Einstein, who is commonly regarded as the most brilliant man of the twentieth century. Although Golding professes not to be able to think himself, the fact that he can read others so well suggests that he must be somewhere between Grades 2 and 1.*

1   While I was still a boy, I came to the conclusion that there were three grades of thinking; and since I was later to claim thinking as my hobby, I came to an even stranger conclusion—namely, that I myself could not think at all.

2   I must have been an unsatisfactory child for grownups to deal with. I remember how incomprehensible they appeared to me at first, but not, of course, how I appeared to them. It was the headmaster of my grammar school who first brought the subject of thinking before me—though neither in the way, nor with the result he intended. He had some statuettes in his study. They stood on a high cupboard behind his desk. One was a lady wearing nothing but a bath towel. She seemed frozen in an eternal panic lest the bath towel slip down any farther, and since she had no arms, she was in an unfortunate position to pull the towel up again. Next to her, crouched the statuette of a leopard, ready to spring down at the top drawer of a filing cabinet labeled A–AH. My innocence interpreted this as the victim's last, despairing cry. Beyond the leopard was a naked, muscular gentleman, who sat, looking down, with his chin on his fist and his elbow on his knee. He seemed utterly miserable.

3   Some time later, I learned about these statuettes. The headmaster had placed them where they would face delinquent children, because they

---

"Thinking as a Hobby" by William Golding from HOLIDAY, July 18, 1961.

symbolized to him the whole of life. The naked lady was the Venus of Milo. She was Love. She was not worried about the towel. She was just busy being beautiful. The leopard was Nature, and he was being natural. The naked, muscular gentleman was not miserable. He was Rodin's Thinker, an image of pure thought. It is easy to buy small plaster models of what you think life is like.

4   I had better explain that I was a frequent visitor to the headmaster's study, because of the latest thing I had done or left undone. As we now say, I was not integrated. I was, if anything, disintegrated; and I was puzzled. Grownups never made sense. Whenever I found myself in a penal position before the headmaster's desk, with the statuettes glimmering whitely above him, I would sink my head, clasp my hands behind my back and writhe one shoe over the other.

5   The headmaster would look opaquely at me through flashing spectacles. "What are we going to do with you?"

6   Well, what *were* they going to do with me? I would writhe my shoe some more and stare down at the worn rug.

7   "Look up, boy! Can't you look up?"

8   Then I would look up at the cupboard, where the naked lady was frozen in her panic and the muscular gentleman contemplated the hindquarters of the leopard in endless gloom. I had nothing to say to the headmaster. His spectacles caught the light so that you could see nothing human behind them. There was no possibility of communication.

9   "Don't you ever think at all?"

10   No, I didn't think, wasn't thinking, couldn't think—I was simply waiting in anguish for the interview to stop.

11   "Then you'd better learn—hadn't you?"

12   On one occasion the headmaster leaped to his feet, reached up and plonked Rodin's masterpiece on the desk before me.

13   "That's what a man looks like when he's really thinking."

14   I surveyed the gentleman without interest or comprehension.

15   "Go back to your class."

16   Clearly there was something missing in me. Nature had endowed the rest of the human race with a sixth sense and left me out. This must be so, I mused, on my way back to the class, since whether I had broken a window, or failed to remember Boyle's Law, or been late for school, my teachers produced me one, adult answer: "Why can't you think?"

17   As I saw the case, I had broken the window because I had tried to hit Jack Arney with a cricket ball and missed him; I could not remember Boyle's Law because I had never bothered to learn it; and I was late for school because I preferred looking over the bridge into the river. In fact, I

was wicked. Were my teachers, perhaps, so good that they could not understand the depths of my depravity? Were they clear, untormented people who could direct their every action by this mysterious business of thinking? The whole thing was incomprehensible. In my earlier years, I found even the statuette of the Thinker confusing. I did not believe any of my teachers were naked, ever. Like someone born deaf, but bitterly determined to find out about sound, I watched my teachers to find out about thought.

18 There was Mr. Houghton. He was always telling me to think. With a modest satisfaction, he would tell me that he had thought a bit himself. Then why did he spend so much time drinking? Or was there more sense in drinking than there appeared to be? But if not, and if drinking were in fact ruinous to health—and Mr. Houghton was ruined, there was no doubt about that—why was he always talking about the clean life and the virtues of fresh air? He would spread his arms wide with the action of a man who habitually spent his time striding along mountain ridges.

19 "Open air does me good, boys—I know it!"

20 Sometimes, exalted by his own oratory, he would leap from his desk and hustle us outside into a hideous wind.

21 "Now, boys! Deep breaths! Feel it right down inside you—huge draughts of God's good air!"

22 He would stand before us, rejoicing in his perfect health, an open-air man. He would put his hands on his waist and take a tremendous breath. You could hear the wind, trapped in the cavern of his chest and struggling with all the unnatural impediments. His body would reel with shock and his ruined face go white at the unaccustomed visitation. He would stagger back to his desk and collapse there, useless for the rest of the morning.

23 Mr. Houghton was given to high-minded monologues about the good life, sexless and full of duty. Yet in the middle of one of these monologues, if a girl passed the window, tapping along on her neat little feet, he would interrupt his discourse, his neck would turn of itself and he would watch her out of sight. In this instance, he seemed to me ruled not by thought but by an invisible and irresistible spring in his nape.

24 His neck was an object of great interest to me. Normally it bulged a bit over his collar. But Mr. Houghton had fought in the First World War alongside both Americans and French, and had come—by who knows what illogic?—to a settled detestation of both countries. If either country happened to be prominent in current affairs, no argument could make Mr. Houghton think well of it. He would bang the desk, his neck would bulge still further and go red. "You can say what you like," he would cry, "but I've thought about this—and I know what I think!"

25   Mr. Houghton thought with his neck.

26   There was Miss Parsons. She assured us that her dearest wish was our welfare, but I knew even then, with the mysterious clairvoyance of childhood, that what she wanted most was the husband she never got. There was Mr. Hands—and so on.

27   I have dealt at length with my teachers because this was my introduction to the nature of what is commonly called thought. Through them I discovered that thought is often full of unconscious prejudice, ignorance and hypocrisy. It will lecture on disinterested purity while its neck is being remorselessly twisted toward a skirt. Technically, it is about as proficient as most businessmen's golf, as honest as most politicians' intentions, or—to come near my own preoccupation—as coherent as most books that get written. It is what I came to call grade-three thinking, though more properly, it is feeling, rather than thought.

28   True, often there is a kind of innocence in prejudices, but in those days I viewed grade-three thinking with an intolerant contempt and an incautious mockery. I delighted to confront a pious lady who hated the Germans with the proposition that we should love our enemies. She taught me a great truth in dealing with grade-three thinkers; because of her, I no longer dismiss lightly a mental process which for nine-tenths of the population is the nearest they will ever get to thought. They have immense solidarity. We had better respect them, for we are outnumbered and surrounded. A crowd of grade-three thinkers, all shouting the same thing, all warming their hands at the fire of their own prejudices, will not thank you for pointing out the contradictions in their beliefs. Man is a gregarious animal, and enjoys agreement as cows will graze all the same way on the side of a hill.

29   Grade-two thinking is the detection of contradictions. I reached grade two when I trapped the poor, pious lady. Grade-two thinkers do not stampede easily, though often they fall into the other fault and lag behind. Grade-two thinking is a withdrawal, with eyes and ears open. It became my hobby and brought satisfaction and loneliness in either hand. For grade-two thinking destroys without having the power to create. It set me watching the crowds cheering His Majesty the King and asking myself what all the fuss was about, without giving me anything positive to put in the place of that heady patriotism. But there were compensations. To hear people justify their habit of hunting foxes and tearing them to pieces by claiming that the foxes like it. To hear our Prime Minister talk about the great benefit we conferred on India by jailing people like Pandit Nehru and Gandhi. To hear American politicians talk about peace in one sentence and refuse to join the League of Nations in the next. Yes, there were moments of delight.

30   But I was growing toward adolescence and had to admit that Mr. Houghton was not the only one with an irresistible spring in his neck. I, too, felt the compulsive hand of nature and began to find that pointing out contradiction could be costly as well as fun. There was Ruth, for example, a serious and attractive girl. I was an atheist at the time. Grade-two thinking is a menace to religion and knocks down sects like skittles. I put myself in a position to be converted by her with an hypocrisy worthy of grade three. She was a Methodist—or at least, her parents were, and Ruth had to follow suit. But, alas, instead of relying on the Holy Spirit to convert me, Ruth was foolish enough to open her pretty mouth in argument. She claimed that the Bible (King James Version) was literally inspired. I countered by saying that the Catholics believed in the literal inspiration of Saint Jerome's Vulgate, and the two books were different. Argument flagged.

31   At last she remarked that there were an awful lot of Methodists, and they couldn't be wrong, could they—not all those millions? That was too easy, said I restively (for the nearer you were to Ruth, the nicer she was to be near to) since there were more Roman Catholics than Methodists anyway; and they couldn't be wrong, could they—not all those hundreds of millions? An awful flicker of doubt appeared in her eyes. I slid my arm round her waist and murmured breathlessly that if we were counting heads, the Buddhists were the boys for my money. But Ruth had really wanted to do me good, because I was so nice. She fled. The combination of my arm and those countless Buddhists was too much for her.

32   That night her father visited my father and left, red-cheeked and indignant. I was given the third degree to find out what had happened. It was lucky we were both of us only fourteen. I lost Ruth and gained an undeserved reputation as a potential libertine.

33   So grade-two thinking could be dangerous. It was in this knowledge, at the age of fifteen, that I remember making a comment from the heights of grade two, on the limitations of grade three. One evening I found myself alone in the school hall, preparing it for a party. The door of the headmaster's study was open. I went in. The headmaster had ceased to thump Rodin's Thinker down on the desk as an example to the young. Perhaps he had not found any more candidates, but the statuettes were still there, glimmering and gathering dust on top of the cupboard. I stood on a chair and rearranged them. I stood Venus in her bath towel on the filing cabinet, so that now the top drawer caught its breath in a gasp of sexy excitement. "A-ah!" The portentous Thinker I placed on the edge of the cupboard so that he looked down at the bath towel and waited for it to slip.

34   Grade-two thinking, though it filled life with fun and excitement, did not make for content. To find out the deficiencies of our elders bolsters the young ego but does not make for personal security. I found that grade two was not only the power to point out contradictions. It took the swimmer some distance from the shore and left him there, out of his depth. I decided that Pontius Pilate was a typical grade-two thinker. "What is truth?" he said, a very common grade-two thought, but one that is used always as the end of an argument instead of the beginning. There is a still higher grade of thought which says, "What is truth?" and sets out to find it.

35   But these grade-one thinkers were few and far between. They did not visit my grammar school in the flesh though they were there in books. I aspired to them, partly because I was ambitious and partly because I now saw my hobby as an unsatisfactory thing if it went no further. If you set out to climb a mountain, however high you climb, you have failed if you cannot reach the top.

36   I did meet an undeniably grade-one thinker in my first year at Oxford. I was looking over a small bridge in Magdalen Deer Park, and a tiny mustached and hatted figure came and stood by my side. He was a German who had just fled from the Nazis to Oxford as a temporary refuge. His name was Einstein.

37   But Professor Einstein knew no English at that time and I knew only two words of German. I beamed at him, trying wordlessly to convey by my bearing all the affection and respect that the English felt for him. It is possible—and I have to make the admission—that I felt here were two grade-one thinkers standing side by side; yet I doubt if my face conveyed more than a formless awe. I would have given my Greek and Latin and French and a good slice of my English for enough German to communicate. But we were divided; he was as inscrutable as my headmaster. For perhaps five minutes we stood together on the bridge, undeniable grade-one thinker and breathless aspirant. With true greatness, Professor Einstein realized that any contact was better than none. He pointed to a trout wavering in midstream.

38   He spoke: "Fisch."

39   My brain reeled. Here I was, mingling with the great, and yet helpless as the veriest grade-three thinker. Desperately I sought for some sign by which I might convey that I, too, revered pure reason. I nodded vehemently. In a brilliant flash I used up half of my German vocabulary. *"Fisch. Ja. Ja."*

40   For perhaps another five minutes we stood side by side. Then Professor Einstein, his whole figure still conveying good will and amiability, drifted away out of sight.

41   I, too, would be a grade-one thinker. I was irreverent at the best of times. Political and religious systems, social customs, loyalties and traditions, they all came tumbling down like so many rotten apples off a tree. This was a fine hobby and a sensible substitute for cricket, since you could play it all the year round. I came up in the end with what must always remain the justification for grade-one thinking, its sign, seal and charter. I devised a coherent system for living. It was a moral system, which was wholly logical. Of course, as I readily admitted, conversion of the world to my way of thinking might be difficult, since my system did away with a number of trifles, such as big business, centralized government, armies, marriage . . .

42   It was Ruth all over again. I had some very good friends who stood by me, and still do. But my acquaintances vanished, taking the girls with them. Young women seemed oddly contented with the world as it was. They valued the meaningless ceremony with a ring. Young men, while willing to concede the chaining sordidness of marriage, were hesitant about abandoning the organizations which they hoped would give them a career. A young man on the first rung of the Royal Navy, while perfectly agreeable to doing away with big business and marriage, got as red-necked as Mr. Houghton when I proposed a world without any battleships in it.

43   Had the game gone too far? Was it a game any longer? In those prewar days, I stood to lose a great deal, for the sake of a hobby.

44   Now you are expecting me to describe how I saw the folly of my ways and came back to the warm nest, where prejudices are so often called loyalties, where pointless actions are hallowed into custom by repetition, where we are content to say we think when all we do is feel.

45   But you would be wrong. I dropped my hobby and turned professional.

46   If I were to go back to the headmaster's study and find the dusty statuettes still there, I would arrange them differently. I would dust Venus and put her aside, for I have come to love her and know her for the fair thing she is. But I would put the Thinker, sunk in his desperate thought, where there were shadows before him—and at his back, I would put the leopard, crouched and ready to spring.

Understanding Meaning

1. When Golding was a child, what question did the teachers always ask him when he was in trouble?
2. That question leads him to watch his teachers to find out about thought. What does he find out?

3.   What are the three grades of thought that Golding comes up with? What is one example that he gives of each?
4.   What does Golding mean when he says that he moved from thinking as a hobby to thinking as a profession?
5.   *CRITICAL THINKING.* Can you think of historical or literary characters who are examples of grade-three, grade-two, and grade-one thinking? Explain your choices.

Evaluating Strategy

1.   Why would Golding start his essay by admitting that as a child in school, he was often in trouble? How does that opening relate to the ending?
2.   Notice how Golding gives significance to descriptive details as he recalls his teachers. What is he suggesting when he describes the light reflecting off his headmaster's glasses? What insights does he provide into Mr. Houghton when he describes him? How does Golding link them to physical features?
3.   Mr. Houghton provides an example of grade-three thinking. What example of grade-two thinking does Golding present?
4.   Throughout the essay, Golding makes use of references to the three small statues. How do the movements in the positions of the statuettes relate to the theme of the essay?

Appreciating Language

1.   How would you rate Golding's language and sentence structure on a scale from most informal to most formal? What exactly led you to so rate it?
2.   Locate an example of Golding's subtle humor.

Writing Suggestions

1.   Write an essay in which you explain Golding's three grades of thinking.
2.   Write an essay in which you explain the significance of the statuettes and the various positions in which they are placed. How do they illustrate what Golding is saying about thinking?
3.   *COLLABORATIVE WRITING.* Exchange essays from Writing Suggestion #1 or #2 above with a member of your group. Read each other's essay with this question in mind: Does evidence in the story support this writer's interpretation? Point out any places where the author needs more support or clearer explanation.
4.   Write an essay in which you apply Golding's theory of thinking to a particular form of prejudice or injustice.

STEPHEN JAY GOULD

Stephen Jay Gould (1941–2002) was a paleontologist and a popular professor of biology, geology, and the history of science at Harvard University. His essays for laypeople on scientific topics made those topics accessible beyond the realm of the specialist. For many years he wrote a monthly column for Natural History *magazine. A number of his books are collections of essays. His last two books,* The Structure of Evolutionary Theory *and* I Have Landed: Splashes and Reflections from a Life in Natural History, *were published in 2002, the year of his death.*

Sex, Drugs, Disasters, and the Extinction of Dinosaurs

CONTEXT: *Gould's purpose in this essay is not to explain why the dinosaurs disappeared but to define the methods by which scientists go about forming and testing hypotheses. Accordingly, the three different explanations for the disappearance of the dinosaurs demonstrate the difference between intriguing speculation and empirical investigation.*

1   Science, in its most fundamental definition, is a fruitful mode of inquiry, not a list of enticing conclusions. The conclusions are the consequence, not the essence.

2   My greatest unhappiness with most popular presentations of science concerns their failure to separate fascinating claims from the methods that scientists use to establish the facts of nature. Journalists, and the public, thrive on controversial and stunning statements. But science is, basically, a way of knowing—in P. B. Medawar's apt words, "the art of the soluble." If the growing corps of popular science writers would focus on *how* scientists develop and defend those fascinating claims, they would make their greatest possible contribution to public understanding.

3   Consider three ideas, proposed in perfect seriousness to explain that greatest of all titillating puzzles—the extinction of dinosaurs. Since these three notions invoke the primally fascinating themes of our culture—sex, drugs, and violence—they surely reside in the category of fascinating claims. I want to show why two of them rank as silly speculation, while the other represents science at its grandest and most useful.

4   Science works with the testable proposals. If, after much compilation and scrutiny of data, new information continues to affirm a hypothesis, we may accept it provisionally and gain confidence as further evidence mounts. We

"Sex, Drugs, Disasters, and the Extinction of Dinosaurs" by Stephen Jay Gould from THE FLAMINGO'S SMILE. NY: W. W. Norton & Co.

can never be completely sure that a hypothesis is right, though we may be able to show with confidence that it is wrong. The best scientific hypotheses are also generous and expansive: They suggest extensions and implications that enlighten related, and even far distant, subjects. Simply consider how the idea of evolution has influenced virtually every intellectual field.

5   Useless speculation, on the other hand, is restrictive. It generates no testable hypothesis, and offers no way to obtain potentially refuting evidence. Please note that I am not speaking of truth or falsity. The speculation may well be true; still, if it provides, in principle, no material for affirmation or rejection, we can make nothing of it. It must simply stand forever as an intriguing idea. Useless speculation turns in on itself and leads nowhere; good science, containing both seeds for its potential refutation and implications for more and different testable knowledge, reaches out. But, enough preaching. Let's move on to dinosaurs, and the three proposals for their extinction.

1. **Sex:** Testes function only in a narrow range of temperature (those of mammals hang externally in a scrotal sac because internal body temperatures are too high for their proper function). A worldwide rise in temperature at the close of the Cretaceous period caused the testes of dinosaurs to stop functioning and led to their extinction by sterilization of males.

2. **Drugs:** Angiosperms (flowering plants) first evolved toward the end of the dinosaurs' reign. Many of these plants contain psychoactive agents, avoided by mammals today as a result of their bitter taste. Dinosaurs had neither means to taste the bitterness nor livers effective enough to detoxify the substances. They died of massive overdoses.

3. **Disasters:** A large comet or asteroid struck the earth some 65 million years ago, lofting a cloud of dust into the sky and blocking sunlight, thereby suppressing photosynthesis and so drastically lowering world temperatures that dinosaurs and hosts of other creatures became extinct.

6   Before analyzing these three tantalizing statements, we must establish a basic ground rule often violated in proposals for the dinosaurs' demise. *There is no separate problem of the extinction of dinosaurs.* Too often we divorce specific events from their wider contexts and systems of cause and effect. The fundamental fact of dinosaur extinction is its synchrony with the demise of so many other groups across a wide range of habitats, from terrestrial to marine.

7   The history of life has been punctuated by brief episodes of mass extinction. A recent analysis by University of Chicago paleontologists Jack Sepkoski and Dave Raup, based on the best and most exhaustive tabulation of data ever assembled, shows clearly that five episodes of mass dying stand well above the "background" extinctions of normal times (when we consider all

mass extinctions, large and small, they seem to fall in a regular 26-million-year cycle). The Cretaceous debacle, occurring 65 million years ago and separating the Mesozoic and Cenozoic eras of our geological time scale, ranks prominently among the five. Nearly all the marine plankton (single-celled floating creatures) died with geological suddenness; among marine invertebrates, nearly 15 percent of all families perished, including many previously dominant groups, especially the ammonites (relatives of squids in coiled shells). On land, the dinosaurs disappeared after more than 100 million years of unchallenged domination.

8   In this context, speculations limited to dinosaurs alone ignore the larger phenomenon. We need a coordinated explanation for a system of events that includes the extinction of dinosaurs as one component. Thus it makes little sense, though it may fuel our desire to view mammals as inevitable inheritors of the earth, to guess that dinosaurs died because small mammals ate their eggs (a perennial favorite among untestable speculations). It seems most unlikely that some disaster peculiar to dinosaurs befell these massive beasts—and that the debacle happened to strike just when one of history's five great dyings had enveloped the earth for completely different reasons.

9   The testicular theory, an old favorite from the 1940s, had its root in an interesting and thoroughly respectable study of temperature tolerances in the American alligator, published in the staid *Bulletin of the American Museum of Natural History* in 1946 by three experts on living and fossil reptiles—E. H. Colbert, my own first teacher in paleontology; R. B. Cowles; and C. M. Bogert.

10   The first sentence of their summary reveals a purpose beyond alligators: "This report describes an attempt to infer the reactions of extinct reptiles, especially the dinosaurs, to high temperatures as based upon reactions observed in the modern alligator." They studied, by rectal thermometry, the body temperatures of alligators under changing conditions of heating and cooling. (Well, let's face it, you wouldn't want to try sticking a thermometer under a 'gator's tongue.) The predictions under test go way back to an old theory first stated by Galileo in the 1630s—the unequal scaling of surfaces and volumes. As an animal, or any object, grows (provided its shape doesn't change), surface areas must increase more slowly than volumes—since surfaces get larger as length squared, while volumes increase much more rapidly, as length cubed. Therefore, small animals have high ratios of surface to volume, while large animals cover themselves with relatively little surface.

11   Among cold-blooded animals lacking any physiological mechanism for keeping their temperatures constant, small creatures have a hell of a time

keeping warm—because they lose so much heat through their relatively large surfaces. On the other hand, large animals, with their relatively small surfaces, may lose heat so slowly that, once warm, they may maintain effectively constant temperatures against ordinary fluctuations of climate. (In fact, the resolution of the "hot-blooded dinosaur" controversy that burned so brightly a few years back may simply be that, while large dinosaurs possessed no physiological mechanism for constant temperature, and were not therefore warm-blooded in the technical sense, their large size and relatively small surface area kept them warm.)

12   Colbert, Cowles, and Bogert compared the warming rates of small and large alligators. As predicted, the small fellows heated up (and cooled down) more quickly. When exposed to a warm sun, a tiny 50-gram (1.76-ounce) alligator heated up one degree Celsius every minute and a half, while a large alligator, 260 times bigger at 13,000 grams (28.7 pounds), took seven and a half minutes to gain a degree. Extrapolating up to an adult 10-ton dinosaur, they concluded that a one-degree rise in body temperature would take eighty-six hours. If large animals absorb heat so slowly (through their relatively small surfaces), they will also be unable to shed any excess heat gained when temperatures rise above a favorable level.

13   The authors then guessed that large dinosaurs lived at or near their optimum temperatures; Cowles suggested that a rise in global temperatures just before the Cretaceous extinction caused the dinosaurs to heat up beyond their optimal tolerance—and, being so large, they couldn't shed the unwanted heat. (In a most unusual statement within a scientific paper, Colbert and Bogert then explicitly disavowed this speculative extension of their empirical work on alligators.) Cowles conceded that this excess heat probably wasn't enough to kill or even to enervate the great beasts, but since testes often function only within a narrow range of temperature, he proposed that this global rise might have sterilized all the males, causing extinction by natural contraception.

14   The overdose theory has recently been supported by UCLA psychiatrist Ronald K. Siegel. Siegel has gathered, he claims, more than 2,000 records of animals who, when given access, administer various drugs to themselves—from a mere swig of alcohol to massive doses of the big H. Elephants will swill the equivalent of twenty beers at a time, but do not like alcohol in concentrations greater than 7 percent. In a silly bit of anthropocentric speculation, Siegel states that "elephants drink, perhaps, to forget . . . the anxiety produced by shrinking rangeland and the competition for food."

15   Since fertile imaginations can apply almost any hot idea to the extinction of dinosaurs, Siegel found a way. Flowering plants did not evolve until late in the dinosaurs' reign. These plants also produced an array of aromatic, amino-acid-based alkaloids—the major group of psychoactive agents. Most mammals are "smart" enough to avoid these potential poisons. The alkaloids simply don't taste good (they are bitter); in any case, we mammals have livers happily supplied with the capacity to detoxify them. But, Siegel speculates, perhaps dinosaurs could neither taste the bitterness nor detoxify the substances once ingested. He recently told members of the American Psychological Association: "I'm not suggesting that all dinosaurs OD'd on plant drugs, but it certainly was a factor." He also argued that death by overdose may help explain why so many dinosaur fossils are found in contorted positions. (Do not go gentle into that good night.)

16   Extraterrestrial catastrophes have long pedigrees in the popular literature of extinction, but the subject exploded again in 1979, after a long lull, when the father-son, physicist-geologist team of Luis and Walter Alvarez proposed that an asteroid, some 10 km in diameter, struck the earth 65 million years ago (comets, rather than asteroids, have since gained favor. Good science is self-corrective).

17   The force of such a collision would be immense, greater by far than the megatonnage of all the world's nuclear weapons. In trying to reconstruct a scenario that would explain the simultaneous dying of dinosaurs on land and so many creatures in the sea, the Alvarezes proposed that a gigantic dust cloud, generated by particles blown aloft in the impact, would so darken the earth that photosynthesis would cease and temperatures drop precipitously. (Rage, rage against the dying of the light.) The single-celled photosynthetic oceanic plankton, with life cycles measured in weeks, would perish outright, but land plants might survive through the dormancy of their seeds (land plants were not much affected by the Cretaceous extinction, and any adequate theory must account for the curious pattern of differential survival). Dinosaurs would die by starvation and freezing; small, warm-blooded mammals, with more modest requirements for food and better regulation of body temperature, would squeak through. "Let the bastards freeze in the dark," as bumper stickers of our chauvinistic neighbors in sunbelt states proclaimed several years ago during the Northeast's winter oil crisis.

18   All three theories, testicular malfunction, psychoactive overdosing, and asteroidal zapping, grab our attention mightily. As pure phenomenology, they rank about equally high on any hit parade of primal fascination. Yet one represents expansive science, the others restrictive and untestable

speculation. The proper criterion lies in evidence and methodology; we must probe behind the superficial fascination of particular claims.

19   How could we possibly decide whether the hypothesis of testicular frying is right or wrong? We would have to know things that the fossil record cannot provide. What temperatures were optimal for dinosaurs? Could they avoid the absorption of excess heat by staying in the shade, or in caves? At what temperatures did their testicles cease to function? Were late Cretaceous climates ever warm enough to drive the internal temperatures of dinosaurs close to this ceiling? Testicles simply don't fossilize, and how could we infer their temperature tolerances even if they did? In short, Cowles's hypothesis is only an intriguing speculation leading nowhere. The most damning statement against it appeared right in the conclusion of Colbert, Cowles, and Bogert's paper, when they admitted: "It is difficult to advance any definite arguments against the hypothesis." My statement may seem paradoxical—isn't a hypothesis really good if you can't devise any arguments against it? Quite the contrary. It is simply untestable and unusable.

20   Siegel's overdosing has even less going for it. At least Cowles extrapolated his conclusion from some good data on alligators. And he didn't completely violate the primary guideline of siting dinosaur extinction in the context of a general mass dying—for rise in temperature could be the root cause of a general catastrophe, zapping dinosaurs by testicular malfunction and different groups for other reasons. But Siegel's speculation cannot touch the extinction of ammonites or oceanic plankton (diatoms make their own food with good sweet sunlight; they don't OD on the chemicals of terrestrial plants). It is simply a gratuitous, attention-grabbing guess. It cannot be tested, for how can we know what dinosaurs tasted and what their livers could do? Livers don't fossilize any better than testicles.

21   The hypothesis doesn't even make any sense in its own context. Angiosperms were in full flower ten million years before dinosaurs went the way of all flesh. Why did it take so long? As for the pains of a chemical death recorded in contortions of fossils, I regret to say (or rather I'm pleased to note for the dinosaurs' sake) that Siegel's knowledge of geology must be a bit deficient: muscles contract after death and geological strata rise and fall with motions of the earth's crust after burial—more than enough reason to distort a fossil's pristine appearance.

22   The impact story, on the other hand, has a sound basis in evidence. It can be tested, extended, refined, and, if wrong, disproved. The Alvarezes did not just construct an arresting guess for public consumption. They proposed their hypothesis after laborious geochemical studies with Frank Asaro

and Helen Michael had revealed a massive increase of iridium in rocks deposited right at the time of extinction. Iridium, a rare metal of the platinum group, is virtually absent from indigenous rocks of the earth's crust; most of our iridium arrives on extraterrestrial objects that strike the earth.

23   The Alverez hypothesis bore immediate fruit. Based originally on evidence from two European localities, it led geochemists throughout the world to examine other sediments of the same age. They found abnormally high amounts of iridium everywhere—from continental rocks of the western United States to deep sea cores from the South Atlantic.

24   Cowles proposed his testicular hypothesis in the mid-1940s. Where has it gone since then? Absolutely nowhere, because scientists can do nothing with it. The hypothesis must stand as a curious appendage to a solid study of alligators. Siegel's overdose scenario will also win a few press notices and fade into oblivion. The Alvarezes's asteroid falls into a different category altogether, and much of the popular commentary has missed this essential distinction by focusing on the impact and its attendant results, and forgetting what really matters to a scientist—the iridium. If you talk just about asteroids, dust, and darkness, you tell stories no better and no more entertaining than fried testicles or terminal trips. It is the iridium—the source of testable evidence—that counts and forges the crucial distinction between speculation and science.

25   The proof, to twist a phrase, lies in the doing. Cowles's hypothesis has generated nothing in thirty-five years. Since its proposal in 1979, the Alvarez hypothesis has spawned hundreds of studies, a major conference, and attendant publications. Geologists are fired up. They are looking for iridium at all other extinction boundaries. Every week exposes a new wrinkle in the scientific press. Further evidence that the Cretaceous iridium represents extraterrestrial impact and not indigenous volcanism continues to accumulate. As I revise this essay in November 1984 (this paragraph will be out of date when the book is published),[1] new data include chemical "signatures" of other isotopes indicating unearthly provenance, glass spherules of a size and sort produced by impact and not by volcanic eruptions, and high-pressure varieties of silica formed (so far as we know) only under the tremendous shock of impact.

26   My point is simply this: Whatever the eventual outcome (I suspect it will be positive), the Alvarez hypothesis is exciting, fruitful science because it generates tests, provides us with things to do, and expands outward. We

---

[1] *The Flamingo's Smile* (1985), in which Gould collected this essay.—EDS.

are having fun, battling back and forth, moving toward a resolution, and extending the hypothesis beyond its original scope.

27   As just one example of the unexpected, distant cross-fertilization that good science engenders, the Alvarez hypothesis made a major contribution to a theme that has riveted public attention in the past few months—so-called nuclear winter. In a speech delivered in April 1982, Luis Alvarez calculated the energy that a ten-kilometer asteroid would release on impact. He compared such an explosion with a full nuclear exchange and implied that all-out atomic war might unleash similar consequences.

28   This theme of impact leading to massive dust clouds and falling temperatures formed an important input to the decision of Carl Sagan and a group of colleagues to model the climatic consequences of nuclear holocaust. Full nuclear exchange would probably generate the same kind of dust cloud and darkening that may have wiped out the dinosaurs. Temperatures would drop precipitously and agriculture might become impossible. Avoidance of nuclear war is fundamentally an ethical and political imperative, but we must know the factual consequences to make firm judgments. I am heartened by a final link across disciplines and deep concerns—another criterion, by the way, of science at its best.[2] A recognition of the very phenomenon that made our evolution possible by exterminating the previously dominant dinosaurs and clearing a way for the evolution of large mammals, including us, might actually help to save us from joining those magnificent beasts in contorted poses among the strata of the earth.

------

[2] This quirky connection so tickles my fancy that I break my own strict rule about eliminating redundancies from [this essay]. . . . —GOULD'S NOTE.

Understanding Meaning

1. How is a valid scientific hypothesis different from what Gould calls "useless speculation"?
2. What does Gould mean when he says in paragraph 5, *There is no separate problem of the extinction of dinosaurs*?
3. What are the three theories about the extinction of dinosaurs that Gould discusses? Why does he consider two of them useless speculation?
4. Why does Gould view the disaster theory as fruitful?
5. *CRITICAL THINKING.* Can you think of other theories that are expansive in the way that Gould describes? That is, are there other theories that expand outward beyond their original scope to provide exciting new knowledge? Explain.

Evaluating Strategy

1. What point does Gould make in paragraphs 5–7 that would be a good rule for all writers of cause and effect analysis to remember?
2. How would you describe the way in which Gould's discussion of the three theories is organized?
3. Gould makes use of a large number of parentheses. What sorts of information does he provide in the parentheses? Are they always used for the same purpose?
4. *BLENDING THE MODES.* Explain how Gould's essay is a blend of cause and effect and examples.

Appreciating Language

1. Gould was a scientist who tried to make science accessible to the layperson. Are there places in this essay where he uses a vocabulary so specialized that his ideas are difficult to understand? Does he sometimes provide enough information to clarify definitions without your having to use a dictionary?
2. Where is some specific language that shows that Gould has a sense of humor about his science?

Writing Suggestions

1. Write an essay in which you explain another scientific hypothesis that may not be provable but that has proved or may prove fruitful in the same sense as Gould explains the disaster theory of the extinction of dinosaurs has been fruitful.
2. *COLLABORATIVE WRITING.* Exchange with a classmate the draft that you wrote for Writing Suggestion #1 above. Have that classmate underline any passages that would not be clear to a college student who is not a specialist in the field you are discussing.
3. Write an essay in which you explain why lab work in science classes is an important supplement to lectures. Be sure to use examples.

ARTHUR JONES

Arthur Jones is editor-at-large for the National Catholic Reporter *and a contributor to the* Tablet, *England's leading Catholic weekly. His book* New Catholics for a New Century *was published in 2000.*

America's Invisible Poor

CONTEXT: *In the following article, which appeared in the April 30, 1999, issue of the* National Catholic Reporter, *Jones challenges the notion that a strong economy is all that is needed to combat poverty. In the midst of a bullish stock market and a brief period of surpluses in the federal budget, the gap between America's rich and poor grew ever larger.*

1   In 1964 the United States government, at the urging of President Lyndon B. Johnson, declared an "unconditional war on poverty."

2   Thirty-two years later, in 1996, the Clinton administration and the U.S. Congress—in the eyes of many antipoverty activists—declared war on the poor.

3   Johnson's decision to combat poverty and his ability to persuade Congress to go along with him was in major part based on a personal concern for the poor and in minor measure a continuation of the legacy of President John F. Kennedy.

4   Kennedy's attitude toward the poor in America had been greatly influenced by social critic Michael Harrington's 1962 book, *The Other America: Poverty in the United States,* a landmark work that drew the nation's attention to the extent of poverty throughout the country.

5   By contrast, Clinton's decision to accede to a conservative Congress' anti-welfare, antipoor initiative was electoral politics, a move to appeal to centrist and right-of-center voters.

6   If, as the critics put it, a war is being waged against poor people, the weapon Clinton and Congress employ is The Personal Responsibility and Work Opportunity Reconciliation Act of 1996, billed as the means "to end welfare as we know it."

7   The description is proving to be correct: Welfare rolls are down, and the number of poor disconnected from any filament of the now-tattered social safety net is beginning to climb. Overall, how fares America?

8   Spring 1999 figures show the U.S. economy is bounding along as merrily as in 1998. Inflation is low; unemployment is at the lowest level in 29 years; mortgage rates are down, and house sales are up. Some ordinary Americans, who 10 or 15 years ago took a chance and started sticking their money into the right stocks and mutual funds, now are worrying about capital gains and tax offsets. The Dow index has risen past the 10,000 mark and continues to set records almost daily.

9   The top 1 percent of America is becoming wealthier, and to protect their corporate asset wealth, they pay their retainers highly. The Children's Defense Fund, in its 1998 "State of America's Children" report, found that in 1960 the average CEO—corporate executive officer—made 41 times the average worker's wage. In 1998, top CEOs averaged $7.8 million annually, 185 times as much as the average worker. In the past decade, states the Children's Defense Fund, while the nation's poorest fifth of families have lost $587 each in purchasing power, the richest 5 percent added $29,533.

10   Adds the defense fund, "Six years of economic expansion with low inflation and a soaring stock market has not filtered down to the 36.5 million poor people."

11   In addition, the number of extremely poor people, those whose incomes are less than 50 percent of the poverty level, has increased.

12   Federal Reserve Board chairman Alan Greenspan explains the reality behind the appearances.

Wealth at Top

13   The typical view, said Greenspan in a speech given at Jackson Hole, Wyo., last September, is that the booming market has benefited individuals "further down in the wealth distribution. Certainly, while in the 1990s those households are more likely to own stocks and mutual funds than a decade or two ago, the stock market rise did not lead to a rise in the share of stocks and mutual fund assets owned by the bottom 90 percent but suggests a further increase in the concentration of net worth [at the top]."

14   How does the rising stock market concentrate assets? Both through wealthy investors rising with the tide and through corporate managers and owner-entrepreneurs cashing in on their stock options.

15   Financial writer Allan Sloan notes that spring is also proxy statement time when multibillionaires like Michael Dell of Dell Computer (who owns $16.4 billion in Dell stock) and Ted Turner ($7.6 billion in Time Warner stock), can exercise their options. That means they can buy more of

their stock very cheaply as a perk for being successful or canny. If they sell some of that cheaply acquired stock while the market is high, they can buy other assets, thus converting paper holdings in their own corporations into concentrated wealth. And those new options, now turned into stock, are bought up by other wealthy investors, mutual funds and the like.

16   In the Other America—to borrow Harrington's title—almost 37 million Americans, 15 percent of the population, live below the poverty line. According to a just-released two-year study by Network, the Catholic social justice lobby, many of the poor, directed toward the welfare-to-work conveyer belt, are not finding jobs and are losing benefits. Consequently, states Network, at least 1 million children "lack basic necessities."

17   And while some welfare recipients have received adequate training and found decent jobs, the number of them still employed 6 and 12 months later is not encouraging. Even welfare recipients who get jobs may not be better off than before. In Michigan, one of the organizations cooperating in the Network study, Groundwork for a Just World, finds severe hardship among those welfare recipients who have "graduated" to work.

18   "Our findings," said Groundwork's Beverly McDonald, "is that people are cycling on and off work, are making less than $7 an hour, with only 25 percent having health coverage on the job and 60 percent with no benefits whatsoever, not even sick time."

19   For those who made it to jobs, many, she said, "are working nonstandard hours. They're leaving their children with friends and relatives and relocating their children in the middle of the night.

20   "Even where the state provides child care support, it is very hard to get when you work nonstandard, fluctuating hours," McDonald said, "and there's a huge lag between when you had to pay for the care and when you got reimbursed for it weeks later."

States Proclaim Reduced Case Loads

21   All that state governments care about, said Groundwork's Beverly McDonald, is proclaiming reduced welfare case loads. Few state governments track what happens to those who slip off welfare or the welfare-to-work conveyer belt, she said.

22   How does Greenspan see the jobs situation? In the speech last September, he said a rising demand for skilled workers who can "effectively harness new technologies" has been outpacing supply and driving up their wages.

23   He mentioned that "earnings inequality occurs within groups of workers with similar skills," but made no mention of the gross inequalities between men's and women's pay for similar jobs (NCR, March 5).

24   Greenspan also looked at wealth distribution and consumption distribution. Inequality in household wealth, he said, was higher in 1989 than in 1963 but hasn't changed much in a decade—"though that masks the apparent rise in the share of wealth held by the wealthiest families. The distribution of wealth," he said, "more fundamentally than earnings or income, measures the ability of households to consume."

25   Writing on Americans in poverty 37 years ago, Harrington referred to those "maimed in body and spirit, existing at levels beneath those necessary for human decency," and said that they were becoming "invisible."

26   The Personal Responsibility and Work Opportunity Reconciliation Act of 1996, by pretending that lower welfare rolls equate with fewer people in poverty, has provided Americans with an additional curtain to shield from them the sight and condition of the poor.

Understanding Meaning

1. What does Jones believe is the difference between President Johnson's attitude toward the poor and President Clinton's? (What's the difference between declaring war on poverty and declaring war on the poor?)
2. How has the economy changed for Americans between 1996 and 1999? Who is in better shape financially? Who is doing worse financially?
3. According to Jones, how are the jobs working out for those who got them through welfare-to-work? What does Jones suggest is the government attitude toward the problems that these citizens new to the work force are experiencing?
4. *CRITICAL THINKING.* Jones suggests wealthier Americans are happy just as long as they don't have to see the suffering of the poor. Do you feel that is an accurate perception?

Evaluating Strategy

1. In the opening paragraphs, Jones is making use of comparison and contrast. Whom is he contrasting?
2. Are Jones's statistics clear and convincing? Do they persuade you that the successes reported for welfare-to-work are deceptive?
3. Jones is appealing in part to his readers' sense of reason and in part to their emotion. Do you feel it is a successful blend?

Appreciating Language

1. What does Jones mean in paragraph 7 when he says that the poor have been "disconnected from any filament of the now-tattered social safety net"? Explain this metaphor.
2. In the metaphors about the fight against poverty being a war, what is President Clinton's weapon?
3. What does Jones mean when he refers to welfare-to-work as a "conveyor belt" in paragraph 16?

Writing Suggestions

1. *PREWRITING.* Do some quick informal writing about your earliest memories of seeing real poverty. Was it, for example, the first time a beggar approached you on the street or when you saw a homeless person? If you have not had any direct contact with the poor, what are some images that stick in your mind from television or movies?
2. Agencies that help the poor often point out that there is an outpouring of generosity around Christmas and Hanukkah but not enough help the rest of the year. Is it true that those who live in relative wealth would rather forget about the poor except at those times of year when it is traditional to donate to them? Write a brief essay about people's attitudes toward the poor.
3. Do you feel that Americans have lost their desire to help those in need? Defend your answer with specific examples.
4. *COLLABORATIVE WRITING.* Discuss this essay with a group of students and draft a statement agreeing or disagreeing with Jones's view of welfare-to-work. If members disagree, consider drafting opposing statements.

WILLIAM SEVERINI KOWINSKI

William Severini Kowinski is a writer, editor, speaker, and consultant who lives in northern California. He has served as an editor of the Boston Phoenix *newspaper. He has published articles on the arts, the environment, politics, and urban design. Many of his essays have appeared in* Smithsonian *magazine. His 1985 book* The Malling of America, *which analyzes the effects of shopping malls, was republished in 2002.*

Kids in the Mall: Growing Up Controlled

CONTEXT: *The following excerpt from Kowinski's* The Malling of America: An Inside Look at the Great Consumer Paradise *(1985) begins with an excerpt from a novel for teenagers and a true story about a boy's attachment to the mall where he virtually grew up. Only then does Kowinski proceed to more general comments about the effects of shopping malls on America's youth. Although he strives to appear evenhanded, Kowinski's title is an allusion to Paul Goodman's* Growing Up Absurd *(1960), a classic study of youth and delinquency in contemporary American society.*

> Butch heaved himself up and loomed over the
> group. "Like it was different for me," he piped.
> "My folks used to drop me off at the shopping
> mall every morning and leave me all day. It was
> like a big free baby-sitter, you know? One night
> they never came back for me. Maybe they moved
> away. Maybe there's some kind of a Bureau of
> Missing Parents I could check with."
> –Richard Peck
>
> Secrets of the Shopping Mall,
> a novel for teenagers

1   From his sister at Swarthmore, I'd heard about a kid in Florida whose mother picked him up after school every day, drove him straight to the mall, and left him there until it closed—all at his insistence. I'd heard about a boy in Washington who, when his family moved from one suburb to another, pedaled his bicycle five miles every day to get back to his old mall, where he once belonged.

2   These stories aren't unusual. The mall is a common experience for the majority of American youth; they have probably been going there all their lives. Some ran within their first large open space, saw their first fountain,

bought their first toy, and read their first book in a mall. They may have smoked their first cigarette or first joint, or turned them down, had their first kiss or lost their virginity in the mall parking lot. Teenagers in America now spend more time in the mall than anywhere else but home and school. Mostly it is their choice, but some of that mall time is put in as the result of two-paycheck and single-parent households, and the lack of other viable alternatives. But are these kids being harmed by the mall?

3   I wondered first of all what difference it makes for adolescents to experience so many important moments in the mall. They are, after all, at play in the fields of its little world and they learn its ways; they adapt to it and make it adapt to them. It's here that these kids get their street sense, only it's mall sense. They are learning the ways of a large-scale, artificial environment; its subtleties and flexibilities, its particular pleasures and resonances, and the attitudes it fosters.

4   The presence of so many teenagers for so much time was not something mall developers planned on. In fact, it came as a big surprise. But kids became a fact of mall life very easily, and the International Council of Shopping Centers found it necessary to commission a study, which they published along with a guide to mall managers on how to handle the teenage incursion.

5   The study found that "teenagers in suburban centers are bored and come to the shopping centers mainly as a place to go. Teenagers in suburban centers spent more time fighting, drinking, littering and walking than did their urban counterparts, but presented fewer overall problems." The report observed that "adolescents congregated in groups of two to four and predominantly at locations selected by them rather than management." This probably had something to do with the decision to install game arcades, which allow management to channel these restless adolescents into naturally contained areas away from major traffic points of adult shoppers.

6   The guide concluded that mall management should tolerate and even encourage the teenage presence because, in the words of the report, "The vast majority support the same set of values as does shopping center management." *The same set of values* means simply that mall kids are already preprogrammed to be consumers and that the mall can put the finishing touches to them as hard-core, lifelong shoppers just like everybody else. That, after all, is what the mall is about. So it shouldn't be surprising that in spending a lot of time there, adolescents find little that challenges the assumption that the goal of life is to make money and buy products, or that just about everything else in life is to be used to serve those ends.

7   Growing up in a high-consumption society already adds inestimable pressure to kids' lives. Clothes consciousness has invaded the grade

schools, and popularity is linked with having the best, newest clothes in the currently acceptable styles. Even what they read has been affected. "Miss [Nancy] Drew wasn't obsessed with her wardrobe," noted the *Wall Street Journal*. "But today the mystery in teen fiction for girls is what outfit the heroine will wear next." Shopping has become a survival skill and there is certainly no better place to learn it than the mall, where its importance is powerfully reinforced and certainly never questioned.

8   The mall as a university of suburban materialism, where Valley Girls and Boys from coast to coast are educated in consumption, has its other lessons in this era of change in family life and sexual mores and their economic and social ramifications. The plethora of products in the mall, plus the pressure on teens to buy them, may contribute to the phenomenon that psychologist David Elkind calls "the hurried child": kids who are exposed to too much of the adult world too quickly and must respond with a sophistication that belies their still-tender emotional development. Certainly the adult products marketed for children—form-fitting designer jeans, sexy tops for preteen girls—add to the social pressure to look like an adult, along with the home-grown need to understand adult finances (why mothers must work) and adult emotions (when parents divorce).

9   Kids spend so much time at the mall partly because their parents allow it and even encourage it. The mall is safe, doesn't seem to harbor any unsavory activities, and there is adult supervision; it is, after all, a controlled environment. So the temptation, especially for working parents, is to let the mall be their baby-sitter. At least the kids aren't watching TV. But the mall's role as a surrogate mother may be more extensive and more profound.

10   Karen Lansky, a writer living in Los Angeles, has looked into the subject, and she told me some of her conclusions about the effects on its teenaged denizens of the mall's controlled and controlling environment. "Structure is the dominant idea, since true 'mall rats' lack just that in their home lives," she said, "and adolescents about to make the big leap into growing up crave more structure than our modern society cares to acknowledge." Karen pointed out some of the elements malls supply that kids used to get from their families, like warmth (Strawberry Shortcake dolls and similar cute and cuddly merchandise), old-fashioned mothering ("We do it all for you," the fast-food slogan), and even home cooking (the "homemade" treats at the food court).

11   The problem in all this, as Karen Lansky sees it, is that while families nurture children by encouraging growth through the assumption of responsibility and then by letting them rest in the bosom of the family from the

rigors of growing up, the mall as a structural mother encourages passivity and consumption, as long as the kid doesn't make trouble. Therefore all they learn about becoming adults is how to act and how to consume.

12   Kids are in the mall not only in the passive role of shoppers—they also work there, especially as fast-food outlets infiltrate the mall's enclosure. There they learn how to hold a job and take responsibility, but still within the same value context. When *CBS Reports* went to Oak Park Mall in suburban Kansas City, Kansas, to tape part of their hour-long consideration of malls, "After the Dream Comes True," they interviewed a teenaged girl who worked in a fast-food outlet there. In a sequence that didn't make the final program, she described the major goal of her present life, which was to perfect the curl on top of the ice-cream cones that were her store's specialty. If she could do that, she would be moved from the lowly soft-drink dispenser to the more prestigious ice-cream division, the curl on top of the status ladder at her restaurant. These are the achievements that are important at the mall.

13   Other benefits of such jobs may also be overrated, according to Laurence D. Steinberg of the University of California at Irvine's social ecology department, who did a study on teenage employment. Their jobs, he found, are generally simple, mindlessly repetitive and boring. They don't really learn anything, and the jobs don't lead anywhere. Teenagers also work primarily with other teenagers; even their supervisors are often just a little older than they are. "Kids need to spend time with adults," Steinberg told me. "Although they get benefits from peer relationships, without parents and other adults it's one-side socialization. They hang out with each other, have age-segregated jobs, and watch TV."

14   Perhaps much of this is not so terrible or even so terribly different. Now that they have so much more to contend with in their lives, adolescents probably need more time to spend with other adolescents without adult impositions, just to sort things out. Though it is more concentrated in the mall (and therefore perhaps a clearer target), the value system there is really the dominant one of the whole society. Attitudes about curiosity, initiative, self-expression, empathy, and disinterested learning aren't necessarily made in the mall; they are mirrored there, perhaps a bit more intensely—as through a glass brightly.

15   Besides, the mall is not without its educational opportunities. There are bookstores, where there is at least a short shelf of classics at great prices, and other books from which it is possible to learn more than how to do sit-ups. There are tools, from hammers to VCRs, and products, from clothes to records, that can help the young find and express themselves. There are

older people with stories, and places to be alone or to talk one-on-one with a kindred spirit. And there is always the passing show.

16   The mall itself may very well be an education about the future. I was struck with the realization, as early as my first forays into Greengate, that the mall is only one of a number of enclosed and controlled environments that are part of the lives of today's young. The mall is just an extension, say, of those large suburban schools—only there's Karmelkorn instead of chem lab, the ice rink instead of the gym: It's high school without the impertinence of classes.

17   Growing up, moving from home to school to the mall—from enclosure to enclosure, transported in cars—is a curiously continuous process, without much in the way of contrast or contact with unenclosed reality. Places must tend to blur into one another. But whatever differences and dangers there are in this, the skills these adolescents are learning may turn out to be useful in their later lives. For we seem to be moving inexorably into an age of preplanned and regulated environments, and this is the world they will inherit.

18   Still, it might be better if they had more of a choice. One teenaged girl confessed to *CBS Reports* that she sometimes felt she was missing something by hanging out at the mall so much. "But I'm here," she said, "and this is what I have."

Understanding Meaning

1. What does Kowinski say are some of the reasons that teenagers spend so much time in malls?

2. What are some of the disadvantages to spending so much time there, according to Kowinski? What lessons are teens learning there? What are they missing out on?

3. What does Kowinski cite as an example of how mall managers have responded to the presence of so many teenagers?

4. It might seem that having a job in a mall would have positive effects on the teenager. Why is that not necessarily true, according to Kowinski and his sources?

5. Near the end of the essay, Kowinski turns to some of the benefits of time spent in the mall. What are those benefits?

6. *CRITICAL THINKING.* Do teenagers in your hometown hang out at a local mall? If not, does your town have someplace equivalent? Does what Kowinski says in the essay apply to the teenagers who go there? Explain.

Evaluating Strategy

1. In his essay, Kowinski analyzes both causes and effects. Where in the essay does he analyze what causes the presence of teenagers in such large numbers in the malls of America? Which paragraphs most directly address the effects that hanging out at the mall has on the youth?
2. Which paragraphs address the effects on teenagers of having a job in a mall?
3. Mall managers did not originally foresee the extent to which teenagers would spend large amounts of time in malls. What decisions have they made in response to the situation?
4. Does Kowinski come across as a reasonable person, willing to consider both sides of a situation? Explain.

Appreciating Language

1. How does Kowinski establish from the first paragraph that he has chosen a fairly informal style for this piece?
2. Would you consider Kowinski's treatment of the mall culture objective or subjective? Explain. Is the same true of the sources that Kowinski quotes?

Writing Suggestions

1. *COLLABORATIVE WRITING.* Work with your group to brainstorm some of the types of people you tend to see in the average mall. Appoint one member of the group to make a list of the ideas the group generates.
2. Using the list from Writing Suggestion #1 above as a starting point, write an essay in which you categorize some of the types of people you see in the mall.
3. Write an essay in which you explain why you agree or disagree with Kowinski's points about why young people go to malls and what the effects are.
4. Write an essay in which you explain why you and your friends used to frequent malls or still do.

DANIEL A. LASHOF

Daniel A. Lashof received his BA from Harvard University in 1980 and completed his PhD at the University of California-Berkeley in 1987. He is a senior scientist and director of the global warming project for the Natural Resources Defense Council. He has taught environmental science as an adjunct professor at the University of Maryland and has published several articles on climate change.

Earth's Last Gasp?

CONTEXT: *Lashof argues in this 1997 article for* USA Today *that the burning of fossil fuels (principally coal, oil, and natural gas) creates an excess of carbon dioxide, "a gas that traps heat like the glass panes of a greenhouse." This greenhouse effect is resulting in the gradual warming of the Earth's temperature. Over time, this will have a disastrous effect on global ecology and even threaten the continuation of human life itself. Although Lashof contends that scientists agree on these facts, politicians have been cautious about taking the necessary actions to prevent further harm to the environment.*

1   "... Entrenched special interests, such as the coal and oil industries, can be expected to use every tool at their disposal to fight sensible climate policies, regardless of the broad-scale benefits for the economy and the environment."

2   When coal, oil, and natural gas are burned to generate electricity, drive automobiles, run factories, and heat homes, the atmosphere is polluted with carbon dioxide, a gas that traps heat like the glass panes of a greenhouse. Scientists have been observing the buildup of carbon dioxide and other so-called greenhouse gases in the atmosphere for decades with increasing interest and concern. Yet, the problem of human-induced global climate change, or global warming, didn't emerge onto the public agenda until 1988, when a string of unusually hot weather, coupled with the Congressional testimony of NASA scientist Jim Hansen proclaiming "a high degree of confidence" that humans already were changing the Earth's climate, garnered headlines around the country.

3   During the following four years, a string of record temperatures and high-profile reports kept global warming in the headlines. This intense period of publicity and diplomatic activity culminated in the Earth Summit at Rio de Janeiro in June, 1992, where 150 nations signed the Rio Climate Treaty, committing themselves to preventing "dangerous" interference with the climate system.

"Earth's Last Gasp?" by Daniel A. Lashof from USA TODAY, May 1997.

4   A combination of factors conspired to move global warming off the front pages following the Earth Summit. Media coverage and Congressional concern seem to be driven more by how hot it was last summer in the eastern U.S. (less than one percent of the planet's surface) than by long-term global warming trends and considered scientific opinion. When particles injected into the stratosphere by the Mt. Pinatubo volcanic eruption in the Philippines in June, 1991, temporarily cooled global temperatures by about 0.5° C, this apparently took the heat off policymakers as well.

5   Recently, though, the climate issue has made a comeback. By the end of 1994, the Pinatubo plume almost completely had settled, and global temperatures returned to record levels in 1995, just as climate models had predicted at the time of the eruption. Meanwhile, an international panel involving around 2,500 scientists from 130 countries quietly had been preparing an updated assessment of climate change. When the Intergovernmental Panel on Climate Change (IPCC) adopted its final report in the fall of 1995, it made headlines around the world for the conclusion that "the balance of evidence suggests a discernible human influence on global climate." Thus, the consensus of the international scientific community confirms Hansen's testimony, which had helped to launch climate change as a public issue seven years earlier. The panel report also included the following:

6   *Rapid climate change.* The average rate of warming over the next century probably will be greater than any seen in the last 10,000 years if global warming pollution is not controlled. Extrapolating from a wide range of scenarios for future pollutant emissions and the scientists' range of uncertainty about how the climate will respond to a given change in greenhouse gas concentrations, global mean temperature is projected to rise by 1.8 to 6.3° F between 1990 and 2100.

7   *Death and disease.* More than 500 deaths were caused by an intense heat wave that struck the midwestern U.S. in the summer of 1995. Although it is not possible to attribute this (or any other) particular event to global climate change, that is the type of event projected to become more frequent due to global warming. A study of Dallas, Tex., by researchers at the University of Delaware projects that the number of heat-related deaths would rise from an average of 20 per year currently to 620–1,360 per year in the middle of the next century. More outbreaks of infectious diseases, such as malaria and dengue fever, are foreseen as well. A Dutch study estimates that, by the middle of the 21st century, climate change could induce more than 1,000,000 additional malaria deaths per year.

8   *Battered coasts.* Global sea levels are expected to rise by one and a half feet during the next century. This will erode beaches, wipe out many

wetlands, and allow storm surges to penetrate farther inland. In cities such as New Orleans, La., and Galveston, Tex., an increase in sea level will mean shoring up seawalls and dikes in order to prevent flooding. In many areas, protection will not be practical and retreat from the shoreline will be the only viable option.

9   *Floods and droughts.* As a result of global warming, more precipitation would come from intense storms and less from gentle drizzles, increasing the risk of storm damage and flooding. At the same time, warmer temperatures would reduce the amount of water stored in mountain snowpacks and dry soils more rapidly, making drought more likely, especially in the mountain, West, and mid-continental areas.

10   *Insurance crisis.* The string of hurricanes, storms, and floods over the last few years has caused billions of dollars in property damage, depleting insurance industry reserves and threatening major companies with bankruptcy. Before 1980, there had been no individual events that caused insured losses over $1,000,000,000; since then, there have been more than a dozen weather-induced billion-dollar catastrophes. Although burgeoning property values in vulnerable areas are a major factor in the heightened losses, claims have risen as a percentage of insured values. There is great concern in the insurance industry that the frequency of extreme weather events could be increasing. Hurricane Andrew, with $20,000,000,000 in insured losses, combined with other recent catastrophes to put nine U.S. insurance companies out of business. It easily could have been much worse—had Andrew struck just 20 miles to the north, damages would have been $75,000,000,000. The insurance industry has taken note of these risks and is beginning to call for pollution cuts.

11   *Ecological havoc.* The ecological implications of climate change will be more subtle than a hurricane, but may be no less significant. According to the World Wildlife Fund, numerous endangered species currently confined to reserves or small pockets of intact habitat could be pushed over the edge to extinction as suitable climate zones shift out from under protected areas. Migration of alpine species upslope has been reported, and some of these species soon could be pushed off mountaintops. Widespread forest dieback—a condition in woody plants whereby peripheral parts are killed—could occur as projected rates of global warming shift climate zones toward the poles as much as 10 times faster than trees can disperse. In the ocean, measurements of zooplankton abundance off the coast of California show an 80% decline over the last 40 years associated with warmer surface water temperatures and reduced transport of nutrients from deeper layers of the ocean.

12   None of this is to suggest that the exact consequences of unabated climate change can be predicted. Nor would it be responsible to assert that the Chicago heat wave, Texas drought, Alaska forest fires, or any other individual extreme event definitely could be the result of greenhouse gas emissions. Nevertheless, the dimensions of the global warming threat are clear and it would be equally irresponsible to ignore the risk that there is a connection. While we can hope that the climate problem turns out to be less severe than current projections indicate, if we choose not to respond, it is equally likely that things will be worse.

Understanding Meaning

1. The article provides a clear explanation of the greenhouse effect. According to Lashof, what first caused this environmental threat to get wide public attention?
2. Whom does Lashof blame for the fluctuation in American attention paid to global warming over the years?
3. Who comprised the IPCC? What was its major finding?
4. Some authors have predicted dire effects from global warming; others predict no effect at all. Where does this author fall on that spectrum?
5. *CRITICAL THINKING.* Look at paragraph 7, "Death and Disease." Various studies predict that heat-related deaths will rise drastically by the middle of this century. Does Lashof seem to suggest that nothing would be done during that time period to counteract the deadly effect of the increasing heat on human health?

Evaluating Strategy

1. Is the essay easy to follow?
2. What does Lashof do in the second paragraph to help nonexperts understand his subject?
3. Why does Lashof not provide sources for his specific factual information?

Appreciating Language

1. Analyze the play on the words *heat* and *hot* in paragraph 4. Does Lashof make such use of wordplay elsewhere?
2. Based on the language in this article, what would you assume about the audience of *USA Today*? How has this prominent scientist adapted his

language for his audience? Is it "reader friendly"? If you have read other essays on global warming, how does this one compare?

Writing Suggestions

1. Explain in an essay what most surprised you in the summary of the report from the IPCC. Were there effects of global warming that you had never thought of or read about before?

2. *COLLABORATIVE WRITING.* Exchange with a classmate a piece you wrote in response to Writing Suggestion #1 above. Respond in writing to the piece you receive, answering these two questions: Is there a thesis statement that clearly sums up what the essay is about? Is there detailed support for that thesis?

LATIFA

Latifa is the pen name of Rohina Sadat (1980–) who was sixteen when the Taliban entered Kabul and established a strict Islamist state in Afghanistan. Prevented by law from attending school, Latifa kept a journal describing her life under the Taliban. In 2001 she published My Forbidden Face: Growing Up Under the Taliban: A Young Woman's Story. *In 2002 Rohina Sadat was named U.N. International Woman of the Year. She now lives in Paris.*

My Forbidden Face: Growing Up Under the Taliban

CONTEXT: *Latifa's narrative chronicles life under the Taliban, a strict Islamist organization that ruled Afghanistan for six years. The Taliban forbade women from attending school, working outside the home, going to beauty parlors, or even being admitted to certain hospitals. The Taliban banned keeping birds, flying kites, playing chess, listening to music, and displaying pictures of people. Jews and Hindus were required to wear yellow cloth. Women who violated Muslim dress code were beaten. Men accused of homosexuality were publicly executed. Shiite Muslims were persecuted and killed. Latifa's account provides insight into the extremes some Islamists seek to impose on other Muslims.*

1   9 A.M., September 27, 1996. Someone knocks violently on our door. My whole family has been on edge since dawn, and now we all start in alarm. My father jumps up to see who it is while my mother looks on anxiously, haggard with exhaustion after a sleepless night. None of us got any sleep: The rocket fire around the city didn't let up until two in the morning. My sister Soraya and I kept whispering in the dark; even after things quieted down, we couldn't fall asleep. And yet here in Kabul, we're used to being the target of rocket fire. I'm only sixteen years old, but I feel as though I've been hearing that din all my life. The city has been surrounded and bombarded for so long, the smoke and flames of the murderous fighting have terrified us so often, sometimes even sending us rushing down to the basement, that another night in this racket is just part of our daily routine!

2   Until this morning.

3   Papa returns to the kitchen, followed by Farad, our young cousin, who is pale and breathless. He seems to be shaking inside, and his face is taut with fear. He can hardly speak, stammering out words in a series of strange gasps.

"My Forbidden Face: Growing Up Under the Taliban" by Latifa from CURRENT EVENTS, October 25, 2002.

4   "I came . . . to find out how you were. Are you all right? You haven't seen anything? You don't know? But they're here! They've taken Kabul! The Taliban are in Kabul. . . ."

5   He turns back and forth from my father to [my brother] Daoud as he speaks, then gazes at my sister and me in anguish. We've heard terrible things about what the Taliban do to women in the provinces they already occupy. I've never seen Farad in such a panic, never seen such overwhelming fear in his eyes. . . . Petrified, the five of us are speechless.

6   Even after my brother told us he'd seen the white [Taliban] flags, I didn't want to believe the truth. . . . So many times I've heard, read, and preferred to ignore what the government has been telling us about the Taliban: "They imprison women in their own homes. They prevent them from working, from going to school. Women have no more lives; the Taliban take away their daughters, burn villagers' houses, force the men to join their army. They want to destroy the country!" . . .

7   Life can't stop like this on the twenty-seventh of September in 1996. I'm only sixteen and still have so many things to do—I have to pass the entrance examination to study journalism at the university. . . . No, it's impossible that the Taliban could remain in Kabul; it's just a temporary setback.

8   Over and over again, [my sister and I] review everything we know . . . about the Taliban's advance to the gates of Kabul. On television we saw widows, enveloped head to toe in their chadris [a head-to-toe veil], beaten with whips and forced to beg in the streets. Today such things are no longer distant images, news flashes on a TV screen: They are here, and they are only too real. Yesterday afternoon was perhaps my last outing in freedom, my last day as a student. . . .

9   And . . . tonight we must try to sleep in the midst of this nightmare.

10   Dawn on this Saturday, the twenty-eighth of September 1996, has the taste of ashes. . . . I am tired to the bone. I feel a sorrow that weighs down my whole body yet leaves me unable to weep. I just lie on my bed. Why get up? . . .

11   What is there to do? I've already said my prayers on the rug Papa bought me from Mecca. I could read the latest article my friend Saber sent me for the little [newsletter] we put out. A bunch of us have been collaborating on this project—entitled *Fager*, which means "Dawn"—for about two years now, producing a single copy of each issue, which passes around the neighborhood from hand to hand before returning to me in a rather dilapidated condition. . . . But now, what's the use of collecting photos and writing articles about Madonna, poetry, the latest fashion, or a new [movie]? If the Taliban control the media, there won't be anything

for us to glean from the press, which will be censored or cease to exist at all. . . .

12   Eleven o'clock. Radio Sharia [Taliban-controlled radio] comes back on to announce that the prime minister of the interim government, which is composed of six mullahs, has issued the following statement.

13   "From now on the country will be ruled by a completely Islamic system. . . . The new decrees in accordance with Sharia are as follows: Women and girls are not permitted to work outside the home. All women who are obliged to leave their homes must be accompanied by their father, brother, or husband. . . . Men must wear a white cap or turban on their heads. The wearing of traditional Afghan clothing is compulsory. Women and girls will wear the chadri. Women and girls are forbidden to wear brightly colored clothes beneath the chadri. It is forbidden to wear nail polish or makeup. It is forbidden to display photographs of animals and human beings. A girl is not allowed to converse with a young man. Muslim families are not allowed to listen to music. All non-Muslims, Hindus, and Jews must wear yellow clothing or a piece of yellow cloth. All those who break the laws of the Sharia will be punished in the public square."

14   This time they're really killing us, killing all girls and women. They're killing us stealthily, in silence. . . . All women are affected, from the youngest to the oldest. Women may no longer work: This means a collapse of medical service and government administration. No more school for girls, no more health care for women, no more fresh air. . . . Women, go home! Or disappear under the chadri, out of the sight of men. It's an absolute denial of individual liberty. . . .

15   The Taliban need only declare themselves through force the absolute masters of Sharia, the precepts of the Koran, which they distort as they please without any respect for the holy book. In my family we are deeply religious; my parents know what the Sharia means for a good Muslim. The injunctions of the Koran have nothing to do with what the Taliban want to impose on us.

16   The Taliban have already forbidden us to keep photos of animals; soon they will forbid us to keep the animals themselves, I'm sure of it. We have a canary in a cage on the living room balcony, which Papa converted into a glassed-in porch to protect us from the cold and from prying eyes. Our bird sings so sweetly at sunrise.

17   Returning from the mosque, Papa finds me sobbing in my room. . . .

18   "Papa, we have to let the canary go. I want him, at least, to be free!"

19   Opening this cage is a vital symbolic gesture. I watch the canary hesitate before this unfamiliar freedom, take flight in a flurry of wings, and disappear

into the distance in the cloudy September sky. It's my liberty he carries away with him. May God guide him safely to some peaceful valley!

[Latifa goes on to describe her days of "endless tunnels of inactivity. . . ."]

20   I spend most of my time lying down in my room, staring at the ceiling or reading. No more jogging, no more bike riding—I'm slowly turning to seed. No more English classes, or newspapers . . . So that the Taliban won't see the glow of the TV screen after my curfew, my uncle came over to paint the windows of [the rooms that] overlook the street. Now only the kitchen window affords a glimpse of the mosque and the school, where there's nothing to see anymore but a circle of boys around the mullah, reciting the Koran.

21   I can't think of anything to do. Sometimes I wander around my home like a convict taking a tour of her cell. I go sit in an armchair, then on a couch or on the rug. I stroll down the hall to the kitchen, then back to my room. I sit down, stretch out, study the designs on the carpets for a while, try the TV again, go lie down once more. I have never before paid such close attention to the furnishings of the apartment. A breadcrumb on the table attracts my notice. A bird fascinates me. . . .

[Latifa tries on a chadri for her friend Farida, who said to Latifa, "If you ever want to go outside, you'll have to wear one."]

22   I put [a chadri] on to humor [my friend Farida] but also to find out what it feels like inside one of these things. The cloth sticks to my nose, it's hard to keep the embroidered peephole in front of my eyes, and I can't breathe.

23   To turn your head, you have to hold the cloth tightly under your chin to keep it in place. To look behind you, you have to turn completely around. I'm hot, and I can feel my breath inside the tent. I'm tripping over the hem. I'll never be able to wear such a garment. Now I know why the "bottle women" walk so stiffly, staring straight ahead or bending awkwardly over unexpected obstacles. I understand why they hesitate before crossing a road, why they go upstairs so slowly. These phantoms now condemned to wander through the streets of Kabul must have a hard time avoiding bicycles, buses, carts. And a hard time escaping from the Taliban. This isn't clothing; it's a jail cell.

24   If I want to go outside, however, I'll have to give in and wear one. . . . At the moment, there's no way I can bring myself to hide beneath that thing. That tiny barred window grid looks like a canary cage. And I'd be the canary.

Understanding Meaning

1. What was Latifa's immediate reaction to the news that the Taliban had taken Kabul?
2. How did she cope with new restrictions imposed on women?
3. How did the Taliban interpret Sharia, or Islamic law? How did their views differ from those of Latifa's family?
4. Why did Latifa decide to release the canary?
5. *CRITICAL THINKING.* What drives people to religious extremism? Other Muslim organizations condemned the Taliban, warning them, for instance, not to follow through with plans to demolish ancient Buddhist statues in Afghanistan. Despite protests from Muslim scholars, Islamic societies, and mullahs in Iran, the Taliban used rockets to smash the Buddhist figures. Why would any religious group ban music or kite flying?

Evaluating Strategy

1. How does Latifa use narrative elements to create both an accurate record of historical events and subjective reaction?
2. What images create the strongest impressions?
3. *BLENDING THE MODES.* How does Latifa use comparison to develop the narrative?
4. Latifa reproduces the Taliban announcement about Sharia in a long exact quote. Is this more effective than a summary in her own words? Can dramatic statements speak for themselves?
5. How does Latifa use the canary as a device for dramatizing conditions under the Taliban?

Appreciating Language

1. What words and phrases dramatize the plight of women under the Taliban?
2. Prevented from going to school, jogging, or riding a bicycle, Latifa writes, "I'm slowly turning to seed." What does "turning to seed" mean?
3. What words does Latifa use to describe her experiences wearing the chadri?

Writing Suggestions

1. Latifa provides a personal account to a historical event, one that began by watching distant events on television. Write a short diary entry about an event you saw on television that affected you personally. Perhaps news from Iraq involved a unit in which a friend or relative serves. A local news report may reveal something troubling about your school, neighborhood, employer or a local official. Record the event objectively, then state your personal reactions.

2. *COLLABORATIVE WRITING.* This section from *My Forbidden Face* appeared in *The Weekly Reader,* a publication for American schoolchildren. Discuss this article with other students. Do you think this article would teach American children about Islam or create misconceptions? Write a brief statement about how Islam should be taught in our schools.

BERNARD LEWIS

Bernard Lewis (1916–) was born in London and received a doctorate in history from the University of London. In 1938 he became an assistant lecturer in Islamic History at the School of Oriental and African Studies at the University of London. Following service in World War II, Lewis was a history professor at London University from 1949 to 1974. He is currently the Cleveland E. Dodge Professor of Near Eastern Studies at Princeton University. An eminent scholar, he has published over twenty books. His most recent books include Islam and the West *(1993),* Cultures in Conflict *(1994),* The Future of the Middle East *(1997),* The Multiple Identities of the Middle East *(1998), and* What Went Wrong: Western Impact and Middle Eastern Response *(2002).*

"I'm Right, You're Wrong, Go to Hell": Religions and the Meeting of Civilizations

CONTEXT: *In this article, which appeared in the* Atlantic Monthly *in 2003, Bernard Lewis explores the similarities and differences between Christianity and Islam. Lewis, a well-known scholar of Islam, argues that much of the conflict between the two religions stems not from their differences but from many of their similarities.*

1   For a long time now it has been our practice in the modern Western world to define ourselves primarily by nationality, and to see other identities and allegiances—religious, political, and the like—as subdivisions of the larger and more important whole. The events of September 11 and after have made us aware of another perception—of a religion subdivided into nations rather than a nation subdivided into religions—and this has induced some of us to think of ourselves and of our relations with others in ways that had become unfamiliar. The confrontation with a force that defines itself as Islam has given a new relevance—indeed, urgency—to the theme of the "clash of civilizations."

2   At one time the general assumption of mankind was that "civilization" meant us, and the rest were uncivilized. This, as far as we know, was the view of the great civilizations of the past—in China, India, Greece, Rome, Persia, and the ancient Middle East. Not until a comparatively late stage did the idea emerge that there are different civilizations, that these civilizations meet and interact, and—even more interesting—that a civilization has a life-span: it is born, grows, matures, declines, and dies. One can

"I'm Right, You're Wrong, Go to Hell: Religions and the Meaning of Civilization" by Bernard Lewis from THE ATLANTIC MONTHLY, May 2003. Reprinted by permission of Bernard Lewis, Cleveland E. Dodge Professor of Near Eastern Studies, Emeritus.

perhaps trace that latter idea to the medieval Arab historian-philosopher Ibn Khaldun (1332–1406), who spoke in precisely those terms, though what he discussed was not civilizations but states—or, rather, regimes. The concept wasn't really adapted to civilizations until the twentieth century.

3   The first writer to make the connection was the German historian Oswald Spengler. Perhaps influenced by the horrors of World War I and the defeat of imperial Germany, he looked around him and saw civilization in decline. He built a philosophy on this perception, captured in the phrase "the decline of the West"—*Der Untergang des Abendlandes*. His two volumes under this title were published in 1918 and 1922. In these he discussed how different civilizations meet, interact, rise and decline, and fall. His approach was elaborated by Arnold Toynbee, who proceeded with a sort of wish list of civilizations—and, of course, also a hit list. Most recently Samuel Huntington, of Harvard University, has argued that the clash of civilizations, more than of countries or governments, is now the basic force of international relations. I think most of us would agree, and some of us have indeed said, that the clash of civilizations is an important aspect of modern international relations, though probably not many of us would go so far as to imply, as some have done, that civilizations have foreign policies and form alliances.

4   There have been a number of different civilizations in human history, and several are extant, though not all in the same condition. Mustafa Kemal, later known as Ataturk, dealt with the relative condition of civilizations in some of the speeches in which he urged the people of the newly established Turkish Republic to modernize. He put the issue with military directness and simplicity. People, he said, talked of this civilization and that civilization, and of interaction and influence between civilizations; but only one civilization was alive and well and advancing, and that was what he called modernity, the civilization "of our time." All the others were dying or dead, he said, and Turkey's choice was to join this civilization or be part of a dying world. The one civilization was, of course, the West.

5   Only two civilizations have been defined by religion. Others have had religions but are identified primarily by region and ethnicity. Buddhism has been a major religious force, and was the first to try to bring a universal message to all mankind. There is some evidence of Buddhist activities in the ancient Middle East, and the possibility has been suggested of Buddhist influence on Judaism and, therefore, on the rise of Christianity. But Buddhism has not expanded significantly for many centuries, and the countries where it flourishes—in South, Southeast, and East Asia—are defined, like their neighbors, by culture more than by creed. These other civilizations, with

the brief and problematic exception of communism, have lacked the ideological capacity—and for the most part even the desire—for indefinite expansion.

6   Christianity and Islam are the two religions that define civilizations, and they have much in common, along with some differences. In English and in most of the other languages of the Christian world we have two words, "Christianity" and "Christendom." Christianity is a religion, a system of belief and worship with certain ecclesiastical institutions. Christendom is a civilization that incorporates elements that are non-Christian or even anti-Christian. Hitler and the Nazis, it may be recalled, are products of Christendom, but hardly of Christianity. When we talk of Islam, we use the same word for both the religion and the civilization, which can lead to misunderstanding. The late Marshall Hodgson, a distinguished historian of Islam at the University of Chicago, was, I think, the first to draw attention to this problem, and he invented the word "Islamdom." Unfortunately, "Islamdom" is awkward to pronounce and just didn't catch on, so the confusion remains. (In Turkish there is no confusion, because "Islam" means the civilization, and "Islamiyet" refers specifically to the religion.)

7   In looking at the history of civilization we talk, for example, of "Islamic art," meaning art produced in Muslim countries, not just religious art, whereas the term "Christian art" refers to religious or votive art, churches and pious sculpture and painting. We talk about "Islamic science," by which we mean physics, chemistry, mathematics, biology, and the rest under the aegis of Muslim civilization. If we say "Christian science" we mean something totally different and unrelated.

8   Does one talk about "Jewish science"? I don't think so. One may talk about Jewish scientists, but that's not the same thing. But then, of course, Judaism is not a civilization—it's a religion and a culture. Most of Jewish history since the Diaspora has taken place within either Christendom or Islam. There were Jews in India, there were Jews in China, but those communities didn't flourish. Their role was minimal, both in the history of the Jews and in the history of India and China. The term "Judeo-Christian" is a new name for an old reality, though in earlier times it would have been equally resented on both sides of the hyphen. One could use an equivalent term, "Judeo-Islamic," to designate another cultural symbiosis that flourished in the more recent past and ended with the dawn of modernity.

9   To what extent is a religiously defined civilization compatible with pluralism—tolerance of others within the same civilization but of different religions? This crucial question points to a major distinction between two types of religion. For some religions, just as "civilization" means us, and the

rest are barbarians, so "religion" means ours, and the rest are infidels. Other religions, such as Judaism and most of the religions of Asia, concede that human beings may use different religions to speak to God, as they use different languages to speak to one another. God understands them all. I know in my heart that the English language is the finest instrument the human race has ever devised to express its thoughts and feelings, but I recognize in my mind that others may feel exactly the same way about their languages, and I have no problem with that. These two approaches to religion may conveniently be denoted by the terms their critics use to condemn them— "triumphalism" and "relativism." In one of his sermons the fifteenth-century Franciscan Saint John of Capistrano, immortalized on the map of California, denounced the Jews for trying to spread a "deceitful" notion among Christians: "The Jews say that everyone can be saved in his own faith, which is impossible." For once a charge of his against the Jews was justified. The Talmud does indeed say that the righteous of all faiths have a place in paradise. Polytheists and atheists are excluded, but monotheists of any persuasion who observe the basic moral laws are eligible. The relativist view was condemned and rejected by both Christians and Muslims, who shared the conviction that there was only one true faith, theirs, which it was their duty to bring to all humankind. The triumphalist view is increasingly under attack in Christendom, and is disavowed by significant numbers of Christian clerics. There is little sign as yet of a parallel development in Islam.

10   Tolerance is, of course, an extremely intolerant idea, because it means "I am the boss: I will allow you some, though not all, of the rights I enjoy as long as you behave yourself according to standards that I shall determine." That, I think, is a fair definition of religious tolerance as it is normally understood and applied. In a letter to the Jewish community of Newport, Rhode Island, that George Washington wrote in 1790, he remarked, perhaps in an allusion to the famous "Patent of Tolerance" promulgated by the Austrian Emperor Joseph II a few years previously, "It is now no more that toleration is spoken of, as if it was by the indulgence of one class of people that another enjoyed the exercise of their inherent natural rights." At a meeting of Jews, Christians, and Muslims in Vienna some years ago the Cardinal Archbishop Franz Koenig spoke of tolerance, and I couldn't resist quoting Washington to him. He replied, "You are right. I shall no more speak of tolerance; I shall speak of mutual respect." There are still too few who share the attitude expressed in this truly magnificent response.

11   For those taking the relativist approach to religion (in effect, "I have my god, you have your god, and others have theirs"), there may be specific political or economic reasons for objecting to someone else's beliefs, but in principle there is no theological problem. For those taking the triumphalist

approach (classically summed up in the formula "I'm right, you're wrong, go to hell"), tolerance is a problem. Because the triumphalist's is the only true and complete religion, all other religions are at best incomplete and more probably false and evil; and since he is the privileged recipient of God's final message to humankind, it is surely his duty to bring it to others rather than keep it selfishly for himself.

12   Now, if one believes that, what does one do about it? And how does one relate to people of another religion? If we look at this question historically, one thing emerges very clearly: whether the other religion is previous or subsequent to one's own is extremely important. From a Christian point of view, for example, Judaism is previous and Islam is subsequent. From a Muslim point of view, both Judaism and Christianity are previous. From a Jewish point of view, both Christianity and Islam are subsequent—but since Judaism is not triumphalist, this is not a problem.

13   But it is a problem for Christians and Muslims—or perhaps I should say for traditional Christians and Muslims. From their perspective, a previous religion may be regarded as incomplete, as superseded, but it is not necessarily false if it comes in the proper sequence of revelation. So from a Muslim point of view, Judaism and Christianity were both true religions at the time of their revelation, but they were superseded by the final and complete revelation of Islam; although they are out-of-date—last year's model, so to speak—they are not inherently false. Therefore Muslim law, sharia, not only permits but requires that a certain degree of tolerance be accorded them.

14   It is, of course, a little more complicated: Jews and Christians are accused of falsifying their originally authentic scriptures and religions. Thus, from a Muslim point of view, the Christian doctrine of the Trinity and of the divinity of Jesus Christ are distortions. The point is made in several Koranic verses: "There is no God but God alone, He has no companion," and "He is God, one, eternal. He does not beget, He is not begotten, and He has no peer." These and similar verses appear frequently on early Islamic coins and in inscriptions, and are clearly polemical in intent. They are inscribed, notably, in the Dome of the Rock, in Jerusalem—a challenge to Christianity in its birthplace. Jews are accused of eliminating scriptural passages foretelling the advent of Muhammad. Anything subsequent to Muhammad, "the Seal of the Prophets," is, from the Muslim perspective, necessarily false. This explains the harsh treatment of post-Islamic religions, such as the Bahai faith and the Ahmadiya movement, in Islamic lands.

15   Muslims did not claim a special relationship to either of the predecessor religions, and if Jews and Christians chose not to accept Muhammad, that was their loss. Muslims were prepared to tolerate them in accordance with

sharia, which lays down both the extent and the limits of the latitude to be granted those who follow a recognized religion: they must be monotheists and they must have a revealed scripture, which in practice often limited tolerance to Jews and Christians. The Koran names a third qualified group, the Sabians; there is some uncertainty as to who they were, and at times this uncertainty provided a convenient way of extending the tolerance of the Muslim state to Zoroastrians or other groups when it was thought expedient. On principle, no tolerance was extended to polytheists or idolaters, and this sometimes raised acute problems in Asian and African lands conquered by the Muslims.

16   Tolerance was a much more difficult question for Christians. For them, Judaism is a precursor of their religion, and Christianity is the fulfillment of the divine promises made to the Jews. The Jewish rejection of that fulfillment is therefore seen as impugning some of the central tenets of the Christian faith. Tolerance between different branches of Christianity would eventually become an even bigger problem. Of course, the outsider is more easily tolerated than the dissident insider. Heretics are a much greater danger than unbelievers. The English philosopher John Locke's famous *A Letter Concerning Toleration*, written toward the end of the seventeenth century, is a plea for religious tolerance, still a fairly new idea at that time. Locke wrote, "Neither pagan, nor Mahometan, nor Jew, ought to be excluded from the civil rights of the commonwealth, because of his religion." Someone is of course missing from that list: the Catholic. The difference is clear. For Locke and his contemporaries, the pagan, the Muslim, the Jew, were no threat to the Church of England; the Catholic was. The Catholic was trying to subvert Protestantism, to make England Catholic, and, as Protestant polemicists at the time put it, to make England subject to a foreign Potentate—namely, the Pope in Rome.

17   Muslims were in general more tolerant of diversity within their own community, and even cited an early tradition to the effect that such diversity is a divine blessing. The concept of heresy—in the Christian sense of incorrect belief recognized and condemned as such by properly constituted religious authority—was unknown to classical Islam. Deviation and diversity, with rare exceptions, were persecuted only when they offered a serious threat to the existing order. The very notion of an authority empowered to rule on questions of belief was alien to traditional Islamic thought and practice. It has become less alien.

18   A consequence of the similarity between Christianity and Islam in background and approach is the long conflict between the two civilizations they defined. When two religions met in the Mediterranean area, each

claiming to be the recipient of God's final revelation, conflict was inevitable. The conflict, in fact, was almost continuous: the first Arab-Islamic invasions took Islam by conquest to the then Christian lands of Syria, Palestine, Egypt, and North Africa, and, for a while, to Southern Europe; the Tatars took it into Russia and Eastern Europe; and the Turks took it into the Balkans. To each advance came a Christian rejoinder: the Reconquista in Spain, the Crusades in the Levant, the throwing off of what the Russians call the Tatar yoke in the history of their country, and, finally, the great European counterattack into the lands of Islam, which is usually called imperialism.

19   During this long period of conflict, of jihad and crusade, of conquest and reconquest, Christianity and Islam nevertheless maintained a level of communication, because the two are basically the same kind of religion. They could argue. They could hold disputations and debates. Even their screams of rage were mutually intelligible. When Christians and Muslims said to each other, "You are an infidel and you will burn in hell," each understood exactly what the other meant, because they both meant the same thing. (Their heavens are differently appointed, but their hells are much the same.) Such assertions and accusations would have conveyed little or no meaning to a Hindu, a Buddhist, or a Confucian.

20   Christians and Muslims looked at each other and studied each other in strikingly different ways. This is owing in part, at least, to their different circumstances. Christian Europeans from the start had to learn foreign languages in order to read their scriptures and their classics and to communicate with one another. From the seventh century onward they had a further motive to look outward—their holy places, in the land where their faith was born, were under Muslim rule, and could be visited only with Muslim permission. Muslims had no comparable problems. Their holy places were in Arabia, under Arab rule; their scriptures were in Arabic, which across their civilization was the language also of literature, of science and scholarship, of government and commerce, and, increasingly, of everyday communication, as the conquered countries in Southwest Asia and North Africa were Arabized and forgot their ancient languages and scripts. In later times other Islamic languages emerged, notably Persian and Turkish; but in the early, formative centuries Arabic reigned alone.

21   This difference in the experiences and the needs of the two civilizations is reflected in their attitudes toward each other. From the earliest recorded times people in Europe tried to learn the languages of the Islamic world, starting with Arabic, the language of the most advanced civilization of the day. Later some, mostly for practical reasons, learned Persian and

more especially Turkish, which in Ottoman times supplanted Arabic as the language of government and diplomacy. From the sixteenth century on there were chairs of Arabic at French and Dutch universities. Cambridge University had its first chair of Arabic in 1632, Oxford in 1636. Europeans no longer needed Arabic to gain access to the higher sciences. Now they learned it out of intellectual curiosity—the desire to know something about another civilization and its ways. By the eighteenth century Europe boasted a considerable body of scholarly literature regarding the Islamic world— editions of texts and translations of historical and literary and theological works, as well as histories of literature and religion and even general histories of Islamic countries, with descriptions of their people and their ways. Grammars and dictionaries of Arabic, Persian, and Turkish were available to European scholars from the sixteenth century onward. It is surely significant that far more attention was given to Arabic, the classical and scriptural language of Islam, than to Persian and Turkish, the languages of the current rulers of the world. In the course of the nineteenth century European and later also American scholars set to work to disinter, decipher, and interpret the buried and forgotten languages and writings of antiquity, and thus to recover an ancient and glorious chapter in history. These activities were greeted with incomprehension and then with suspicion by those who did not share and therefore could not understand this kind of curiosity.

22   The Islamic world, with no comparable incentives, displayed a total lack of interest in Christian civilization. An initially understandable, even justifiable, contempt for the barbarians beyond the frontier continued long after that characterization ceased to be accurate, and even into a time when it became preposterously inaccurate.

23   It has sometimes been argued that the European interest in Arabic and other Eastern languages was an adjunct—or, given the time lag, a precursor— of imperialism. If that is so, we must acquit the Arabs and the Turks of any such predatory intent. The Arabs spent 800 years in Spain without showing much interest in Spanish or Latin. The Ottomans ruled much of southeastern Europe for half a millennium, but for most of that time they never bothered to learn Greek or any Balkan or European language—which might have been useful. When they needed interpreters, they used converts and others from these various countries. There was no Occidentalism until the expanding West forced itself on the attention of the rest of the world. We may find similar attitudes in present-day America.

24   Today we in the West are engaged in what we see as a war against terrorism, and what the terrorists present as a war against unbelief. Some on both sides see this struggle as one between civilizations or, as others would put it, between religions. If they are right, and there is much to support

their view, then the clash between these two religiously defined civilizations results not only from their differences but also from their resemblances—and in these there may even be some hope for better future understanding.

Understanding Meaning

1. According to Lewis, how did the events of September 11, 2001, reveal a different way people define themselves?
2. How did Christianity and Islam define civilizations? How are Christianity and Islam different than Judaism and Buddhism?
3. How did Christian and Islamic civilizations deal with pluralism? How did they treat those with different beliefs?
4. What distinction does Lewis make between "Christianity" and "Christendom"? Why does the lack of such a division in Islam create confusion?
5. How did Christians and Muslims differ in the way they looked at and studied each other?
6. Is a clash between Muslims and Christians more likely caused by their similarities than their differences?
7. *CRITICAL THINKING.* Who does the concept of a clash between civilizations appeal to? President Bush has repeatedly made statements that the war on terrorism is not an assault on Islam. Several Christian and Muslim authorities, however, have seen the conflict as one between religions, between civilizations. In your view, should the U.S. government embrace or reject this view? Why or why not?

Evaluating Strategy

1. How does Lewis define *civilization*?
2. How does Lewis use historical events to explain the similarities and differences between Islam and Christianity?
3. *BLENDING THE MODES.* Where does Lewis use comparison, definition, example, and cause and effect to develop his essay?

Appreciating Language

1. How do you define the word *tolerance*? Does it suggest to you the meaning Lewis sees—that tolerance assumes that a superior person grants an inferior person limited rights? How does Lewis use George Washington's famous letter about tolerance to establish his definition?

2. Look up the terms *jihad* and *crusade*. What are their objective meanings? What connotations do they have? Why, for instance, did President Bush's initial use of the word "crusade" to describe the war on terrorism receive criticism? Why did he and other officials subsequently avoid using the word?

Writing Suggestions

1. Write a brief essay that defines how you view America's relations with Islam. Do you see a major "clash of civilizations" or simply a clash with a small group of fanatics? Does it have more to do with religion or economics?
2. *COLLABORATIVE WRITING.* Discuss this essay with other students. Do they consider themselves members of a "Christian" civilization? If so, how do they define it? Record reactions of the group. If members have different opinions, consider writing separate statements.

JOHN LEO

John Leo (1935–), associate editor of Time *magazine, has written editorials and commentary for such leading magazines as* Time, Commonweal, *the* New York Times, *the* Village Voice, *and* U.S. News and World Report. *A master of the familiar essay, he writes engagingly on topics of broad interest for an audience of intelligent general readers.*

Enslaved to the Past

CONTEXT: *In the following column, which appeared in the April 15, 2002, issue of* U.S. News and World Report, *Leo predicts that the effort to achieve racial reparations through legislation or through judicial decree is probably doomed to failure. What is likely to happen is that the mere filing of suits will prompt corporations to make settlements out of court in order to avoid bad publicity. This sort of leverage (or intimidation) has often been used effectively by some political figures in their dealings with corporate America.*

1   Polls show that 75 percent of Americans, and 90 percent of whites, are opposed to paying reparations to blacks for the enslavement of their ancestors. This means that the reparations fight will not take place in the political arena, where victory is probably impossible. Instead, it will be a legal and public relations campaign to force corporate America to pay.

2   This is an obvious strategy. Nobody loves corporations, and that's where the money is. So the class action lawsuits for reparations, filed in late March against Aetna, rail network CSX, and FleetBoston bank, are just the first surge of litigation against companies historically linked in some way to the slave trade. The lawyers involved say as many as a thousand large corporations will eventually be sued. Another team of lawyers, including Johnnie Cochran and Harvard law Prof. Charles Ogletree, plans more suits this summer.

3   Will these suits get anywhere in the courts? Probably not. Our modern liberated judges are capable of anything, and juries hand out huge awards for little or no reason. Most experts, however, think the legal case for reparations is weak and fraught with too many obstacles, including a long-expired statute of limitations. But the strategy is to force settlements, not necessarily to win outright in court. Randall Robinson, author of a pro-reparations book, *The Debt*, says: "Once the record is fleshed out and made

fully available to the American people, I think companies will feel some obligation" to settle.

4   This sense of obligation will be enhanced by the possibility of boycotts and terrible publicity during prolonged litigation. The nice way to put this strategy is to say that corporations are being pushed to pay as a reflection of national guilt and an emerging moral consensus. Or you could just say that this is a racial shakedown.

5   Fighting back. The history of this technique is currently on display in the new book *Shakedown*, Kenneth Timmerman's account of the career of Jesse Jackson. Only rarely did a corporation fight back when exposed to the Jackson treatment. (Nike did and won.) In general, corporations are so fearful of the racist label that they prefer to backpedal and pay what amounts to protection money. Ward Connerly and Edward Blum, leaders of the fight against set-asides and racial preferences, recently wrote: "Texaco, Denny's, Coca-Cola, and others have settled specious bias claims rather than have Mr. [Al] Sharpton, Mr. Jackson, and members of the Congressional Black Caucus call for a nationwide boycott of their companies."

6   Many conservatives have the sense that corporate America has trapped itself by capitulating so often and so easily, not just in payouts and buy-offs but in indoctrinating employees ("diversity training") and installing large and unproductive diversity bureaucracies inside their own companies. Perhaps it is too late for a spinal transplant. But the cost of caving in this time would be staggering, possibly in the billions.

7   So far the activists have not made enormous headway, but it's fair to say that reparation is no longer considered the absolutely wacky issue that it was four or five years ago. Sectors of the media are now treating it as a legitimate issue, particularly media companies that have been identified as having some financial tie to slavery in the old days (Gannett, Knight-Ridder, and the *Hartford Courant*, for example).

8   The nudge of guilt is also being applied to another constituency the reparations people will need: the universities. Harvard, Yale, Princeton, Brown, and the University of Virginia have all been identified as having embarrassing connections to slavery. This raises the specter of idealistic students annually denouncing their own universities as racist and demanding pro-reparations action by administrators, the keepers of university stock portfolios, and all those professors on corporate boards. David Horowitz's book *Uncivil Wars* is a revelation about how far some elite campuses were willing to go just to suppress a newspaper ad opposing reparations.

9   So it's possible that the reparations issue could take off. We should all hope it doesn't. This campaign is the work of an aging and backward-looking

black leadership that can't seem to extricate itself from victim politics. The not-so-subtle message is that black Americans are so mangled by the legacy of slavery that they must be paid off massively to compensate for their incapacity. It undermines the positive message that blacks can compete with anyone in any field and rise on their own, without crutches or patronizing handouts. When the issue is reparations, just say no.

Understanding Meaning

1.   Why does Leo feel that reparations for slavery may eventually take the form of out-of-court settlements by corporations? What are some of the reasons lawsuits on the issue are not likely to be won? Why are they not likely to even make it to a courtroom?
2.   Leo is not specific about why Aetna, CSX, and FleetBoston have been targeted for class-action lawsuits. How might these companies have been "historically linked in some way to the slave trade"? What about the universities that Leo later mentions?
3.   What role does Jesse Jackson have in these pending legal settlements, according to Leo? What does Leo mean when he refers to them as a "racial shakedown"? Why have large companies given in to this tactic?
4.   Which parties involved have shown evidence that they are taking the matter of reparations seriously?
5.   Why does Leo feel that we should all hope this issue does not "take off"?
6.   *CRITICAL THINKING.* Consider what you know about the charges that have been made against such large companies as Texaco, Denny's, and Coca-Cola. When you heard about them, did you associate them with slavery in our country? Do you now, now that you have read Leo's article? Are such companies linked with the others that Leo mentions by a shared guilt over slavery or by the tactic used against them by African American leaders? Explain.

Evaluating Strategy

1.   Leo starts his essay with a blunt statement about what percent of Americans are opposed to the paying of reparations for slavery. How does it serve his purpose to present a reparations victory in court as an impossible dream?
2.   Where—and through what specific language—does Leo first reveal his own particular bias on the issue he is discussing? Where does he most bluntly state his opinion about the possibility that corporations will eventually be forced to pay reparations for slavery?

3.   How does Leo's reference to Kenneth Timmerman's book strengthen his argument?
4.   *CRITICAL THINKING.* Part of Leo's strategy is exposing the strategy used by some leaders in the African American community. Do you feel that he builds a convincing case for his condemnation of them at the end of the essay?

Appreciating Language

1.   By the end of the essay, Leo uses some emotionally charged language. What are some examples? Consider the audience for whom he was writing. How might they have responded?
2.   What does Leo mean when he suggests that it may be "too late for a spinal transplant"?
3.   In the last paragraph, how does Leo try to show that he has a more positive view of the ability of African Americans than their own leaders seem to have?

Writing Suggestions

1.   Write a paragraph in which you summarize Leo's article. Be sure not to leave out any major ideas. And be objective. A summary is not the place to express your opinions.
2.   *COLLABORATIVE WRITING.* Before discussing the article in class, exchange paragraphs from Writing Suggestion #1 above and see to what extent you and your classmates focused on the same major ideas.
3.   Write a paragraph in which you evaluate Leo's article. This time you will be expressing an opinion.
4.   *COLLABORATIVE WRITING.* Now exchange this second round of paragraphs and see how much agreement there was.
5.   Write an essay in which you either agree or disagree with Leo's last paragraph.

CARYLE MURPHY

Caryle Murphy (1946–) was born in Hartford, Connecticut, and grew up in Brockton, Massachusetts. She attended Trinity College in Washington and joined the staff of the Washington Post *in the late 1970s. She served as the* Washington Post's *Cairo bureau chief for five years. She was in Kuwait in August 1990 when Iraq invaded the country, forcing her to remain underground for twenty-seven days. Her most recent book is* Passion for Islam: Shaping the Modern Middle East: The Egyptian Experience *(2002).*

The War on Terrorism: Why It Really Will Be a Long One

CONTEXT: *Murphy argues in this essay, published in April 2003, that the situation in the Middle East results from three historical forces: a reawakening Islam struggling with modernity; the West's failure to resolve the Israeli-Palestinian conflict; and the lack of political liberties and authoritarian regimes that "has reduced Arab political life and discourse to an infantile level."*

1   The war now being fought by U.S. military forces in Iraq means that Saddam Hussein's murderous reign is finished. And the recent capture of several senior al-Qaeda operatives gives hope that the terrorist network's lifespan has been considerably shortened. But these developments do not mean that the U.S. war on terrorism will soon be over.

2   Tactical initiatives, like routing the Taliban in Afghanistan and hunting down al-Qaeda, are insufficient to win that war and ensure our long-term safety in what is a very small world these days. What is still missing—and expected of a superpower—is a sophisticated long-term strategy, supported by patience and perseverance, for combating the roots of the religious terrorism that struck our country with such fury on Sept. 11, 2001.

3   For this, we need to understand the reasons for the combustible environment in today's Middle East. This is not excusing terrorism, nor is it a sign of weakness. On the contrary, such understanding fortifies us. Knowledge is power.

4   During five years as a correspondent in the Middle East, I learned that most Arab Muslims do not hate us, though they do hate some of our foreign policies. They certainly do not hate us for our freedoms. This statement tells us very little that is useful in forming U.S. policy or U.S. behavior abroad.

"The War on Terrorism: Why It Really Will Be a Long One" by Caryle Murphy from AMERICA, April 28, 2003. Reprinted by permission of America Press.

Evildoers do indeed exist. But there are social, cultural, political and religious influences that created the conditions that gave rise to groups like al-Qaeda.

5　　　The situation in the Middle East today is the result of the convergence of three major historical forces that have been unfolding for decades: first, Islam's reawakening as it comes to terms with modernity; second, the failure of the international community, in particular the United States, to resolve the long-running Israeli-Palestinian conflict, now more than a half-century old; and third, the lack of political liberties and the authoritarianism of Arab governments that has reduced Arab political life and discourse to an infantile level.

6　　　Most perplexing perhaps for Americans is the revival of Islam, which is unfolding on four distinct but complementary levels. In the daily lives of ordinary Muslims, these levels intersect and overlap. But when examined separately, they illuminate why Islam, a faith grounded in the same monotheistic tradition as Judaism and Christianity, is passing through a historic crucible.

7　　　The first level is pious Islam, by which I mean the increased personal religious devotion seen in millions of Muslims in recent decades. Whether it be stricter observance of fasting during Ramadan, wearing the veil, attending weekly study groups on the Koran or being more conscientious about saying prayers five times a day, this growing personal piety is evident in every Arab country.

8　　　The second level, political Islam, is the one that draws the headlines. But political Islam spans a wide spectrum. At one end are Islamists with a messianic mission to convert the world to their militant version of Islam. They use violence to that end. The prime example is al-Qaeda. At the other end of the spectrum are peaceful political activists, with a more tolerant brand of Islam, who reject violence. We can expect that these opposition activists will continue to use Islam as a vehicle for their activities for some years to come. And we cannot write off all of them as religious fanatics.

9　　　The third level of Islam's reawakening is cultural Islam. Many Muslims feel threatened by the powerful penetration of their societies and cultures by Western, and in particular American, culture—something that has been accelerated by globalization. In response they are returning to their roots, in other words, to Islam. This faith permeates Arab cultural life in a way that no religion, not even Christianity, penetrates Western culture.

10　　　This return to roots, or cultural Islam, is expressed in a variety of ways, some more evident than others. Some young Muslims, for example, reject Western music and films. Others are making an effort to articulate in an Islamic way, or by means of an Islamic vocabulary, values that they have come to identify—rightly or wrongly—as "Western" values: ideas like democracy, individualism, human rights and feminism. They are seeking to blend these values with their own Islamic cultural background and to express them in a way that makes sense within their Islamic world-view.

11   Cultural Islam is constantly in conflict with the allure of American culture. So while thousands of young Arabs love Jennifer Lopez, watch "Dallas" and rent Tom Cruise movies, others shun them. And even within the same person, there are often two colliding impulses. One says, I want to be just like those Americans. The other says, it is humiliating to imitate Americans, whose secular culture is corroding my Islamic culture.

12   The last manifestation of Islam's reawakening, which I call new thinking in Islam, is playing out on the theological level. Often overlooked, it is likely in the long run to be the most revolutionary aspect of this revival. Right now, more Muslims around the world are re-examining their theological heritage than at any other time in Islam's 1,300-year history. For centuries, religious scholars with years of training in Islam's sacred texts were looked to for authoritative interpretations of those texts. Now, to an unprecedented degree, ordinary Muslims are claiming the right to examine and reinterpret those texts themselves.

13   Essentially, Muslims are wrestling with what one young American Muslim scholar called the "interpretive imperative" to make their religion more relevant to modern times. In the process, they are grappling with big questions: What is the relationship between religious knowledge and secular knowledge? How does religious knowledge differ from religion itself? How should Islamic law, or shariah, be applied to contemporary moral and political questions? Who is to judge apostasy in a world where freedom of religious conscience is widely regarded as a basic human right? What is the relationship between political authority and God's sovereignty? And, perhaps most importantly, the key question: What is Islam's role in the public life of a modern Muslim society?

14   We Americans settled a similar question more than 200 years ago. Despite the lawsuits that arise every holiday season as some object to creches or menorahs in front of city hall, we enjoy a very solid national consensus about the role of religion in our country's public life. This is not so in many Muslim countries, where there has always been a close relationship between religion and politics. The Egyptian Constitution, for example, states that Islam is the official religion of the state. As a result, predominantly Muslim countries do not see the "American solution" as appropriate for them.

15   Islam, which has no Vatican, has always been a pluralistic faith of many interpretations. The current theological introspection is invigorating that pluralism, and all over the world thousands of competing voices are each saying, "I have the true Islam," or "This is the way Islam should be lived."

16   Unfortunately, at this particular moment in the Middle East, the more orthodox, more conservative and sometimes more radical voices—often espousing a literalist reading of Scripture—have the upper hand. When societies feel defensive, humiliated and beleaguered—as those in that region of the world do now—they are not at their most creative. At such times, hard-liners usually prevail. The exact opposite situation is evident in Muslim communities in the United States and Europe, where the moderate voices are the dominant ones.

17   It is frightening that some in the United States are taking a simplistic view of this internal struggle within Islam, equating the faith itself with its most radical, violent and anti-Western adherents. These political commentators and Christian leaders are promoting the view that Islam is at war with America, when the reality is that only a faction of radical Islamists is at war with us. In today's world of instant-messaging, insensitive remarks about Islam by people like Franklin Graham, Pat Robertson and Jerry Falwell are transmitted around the world in hours, where they fuel the growing belief that the predominantly Judeo-Christian nation of America is on a "crusade" against Islam. In such an inflamed atmosphere, remarks like these dissipate the goodwill sown by the efforts of Pope John Paul II to promote peace and Catholic-Muslim dialogue.

18   To win the war on terrorism, the United States must turn around the Middle Eastern environment and help moderate Muslims find their voices. But this will not be done on a dime. It is a long-range project that requires changes in U.S. policies—first of all regarding the Israeli-Palestinian conflict, which has bred such resentment and anger toward our country. President George W. Bush's recent presentation of a "road map" to resolve this conflict is a long overdue step in the right direction. But is it genuine? Will it lead to a vigorous, engaged and sustained U.S.-led international campaign to follow the road map to its destination? Or was it just a public relations exercise to pre-empt antiwar sentiment on the eve of the U.S. war against Iraq? Everyone knows what is needed to resolve this conflict in a fair and just way to both sides. The ingredients have been around for a long time. What is missing is the will and determination to implement them.

19   Second, the United States must confront the political frustration and economic disappointments caused by authoritarian Arab governments. It should consistently and publicly criticize human rights abuses by Middle

Eastern governments, including Israel, help improve Arab education systems and encourage political liberalization.

20   If the United States is sincere about promoting democracy in the Arab world, it has to be patient. People accustomed to authoritarianism do not learn new ways of thinking about politics in a year. It also must realize that this process may sometimes be messy, and that elections may bring to power leaders or parties with Islamist agendas. We should be ready to distinguish between such parties—Islamists are not all the same—and judge them by their actions. With their sizeable constituencies, Islamists will likely be part of the solution of moving toward more democratic societies.

21   The United States also must set a good example by preserving the legal and civil rights that have made our country a beacon of freedom around the world. Lamentably, those liberties are being eroded in the name of the war on terrorism, damaging our moral authority to censure abuses in other countries.

22   Transforming the Middle East environment should involve not just our government, but all Americans, who have shown that when asked to contribute to their national security, they can muster a multitude of resources. Businessmen, tourism officials, university professors, scientists, political consultants and not least theologians all need to be recruited to initiate dialogue with their counterparts. The pity is that right now such contacts are diminishing.

23   The U.S. war in Iraq will certainly mark a historic crossroads in Arab-U.S. relations. Whether those relations improve depends not only on how the United States manages post-Hussein Iraq but also on how it addresses the roots of terrorism. Terrorists are a minority, but they win public sympathy because the United States acts arrogantly and is inconsistent in its support for democracy and short-sighted in letting the Israeli-Palestinian conflict fester.

24   If the United States moves strategically to transform the Middle East environment, its efforts will be well received. I know this from the many young Muslims I met there who want to be a successful part of the global community. They are moderate in religion and tolerant of other faiths. They are eager for new thinking in Islam that is compatible with democracy and modernity and that gives them a sense of restored dignity. They know deep down that a closed, cramped version of their faith will not allow Islam to maintain its vibrancy as a spiritual force. These Muslims have one eye on their computer icons and another on their minarets as they search for a

moderate and modern middle way in the Middle East. All we have to do is help them find it.

Understanding Meaning

1. How does Murphy distinguish between America's successful short-term "tactics" in defeating the Taliban and Saddam and its need for a long-term "strategy"?
2. What are the three levels Murphy sees in the Islamic revival?
3. How has the revival of Islam influenced Arab attitudes toward the West? How do young Muslims respond to American popular culture?
4. What, in Murphy's view, is the best way for the United States to win the war on terrorism?
5. According to Murphy, what must the United States do to promote democracy in the Arab world?
6. Why does Murphy believe that a transformation of the Middle East cannot rely on the American government but must engage all the American people?
7. *CRITICAL THINKING.* Murphy points out that many Arabs identify democracy, individualism, human rights, and feminism with the West. Does hostility to Western culture and social behavior make it harder for Arabs to embrace these values? Should democracy and human rights be depicted as something that is international and not "Western"? Would Asian and African advocates of democracy and human rights be more effective in influencing the Arab world?

Evaluating Strategy

1. How does Murphy use classification to explain the Islamic reawakening?
2. Where does Murphy use comparison and contrast to discuss Arab attitudes toward the United States?
3. Murphy mentions that she served as a correspondent in the Middle East for five years. What does this add to her essay? Does it distinguish her from the other commentators who may never have visited an Arab country?
4. How effective is Murphy's conclusion?

Appreciating Language

1. Murphy states that Arab political discourse has been reduced to an "infantile" level. What does this term imply? Can you think of examples of "infantile" political thought?

2. What is the "interpretative imperative" in Islam? Is this an important term for non-Muslims to understand, in order to appreciate the intellectual and theological conflicts among Islamic scholars?
3. How does Murphy define "pious Islam," "political Islam," and "cultural Islam"? Why are these distinctions important?

Writing Suggestions

1. Based on Murphy's observations, write a brief essay outlining ways that Americans could help moderate Muslims find their voices. Can the United States try to influence other nations without appearing to be patronizing or condescending?
2. *COLLABORATIVE WRITING.* Discuss with other students Murphy's classification of the different aspects of the Muslim revival. Work together to summarize her points in a single paragraph that would help explain the complexity of Islam for a high school history textbook.

ANNA QUINDLEN

Anna Quindlen (1952–) graduated from Barnard College in 1974 and began working as a reporter in New York. After writing articles for the New York Post, *she took over the "About New York" column for the* New York Times. *In 1986 she started her own column, "Life in the Thirties." Her collected articles were published in* Living Out Loud *in 1988. She has written numerous op-ed pieces for the* Times *on social and political issues. In 1992 she received the Pulitzer Prize. The following year she published another collection of essays,* Thinking Out Loud: On the Personal, the Political, the Public, and the Private *(1994).* Quindlen has also written three novels: Object Lessons *(1991),* One True Thing *(1995), and* Black and Blue *(1998).*

Out of the Time Warp

CONTEXT: *In January 1973, a 7–2 majority of the United States Supreme Court ruled that a woman's constitutional right to privacy severely limited the ability of the government to restrict abortion. Thirty years (and 27 million legal abortions) later, Anna Quindlen looks back on this historic decision* (Roe v. Wade) *in her biweekly column in* Newsweek. *Quindlen argues that the decision greatly altered the role of women in society by making motherhood a matter of choice. She also seems to suggest that these changed circumstances allowed women to see for the first time how demanding a job motherhood could be, and how immoral it would be to force such a burden on a woman who did not desire it.*

1   The must-see movies were *The Poseidon Adventure* and *Deliverance*. The average new car cost more than $4,000. "You're So Vain" was the No. 1 single on the record charts. Airlines began a new practice: inspecting carry-on luggage.

2   It was the beginning of 1973, and in some ways it seems a very long time ago. Yet the most important event of that period is somehow frozen in amber. Thirty years ago this week the Supreme Court ruled that American women had a constitutional right to privacy that included legal abortion. *Roe v. Wade* has become the starting point for every discussion about the issue ever since.

3   How Americans feel has changed very little in polls over the past three decades. According to Gallup, "Americans believe abortion should be legal, but on a somewhat limited basis." But everything has changed in the lives of American women. Those changes will set the stage for abortion politics

in the years to come, at least as much as—perhaps more than—the decades-old decision of the high court.

4   The impulse to combine the world at home with the world of work is not an option today; it is a given. There are women for whom a career is an essential part of identity and self-esteem. There are women for whom a job is an essential part of buying groceries and paying rent. And there are women for whom trading a welfare check for a minimum-wage job is an essential part of government reform programs.

5   The number of mothers working outside the home has grown incrementally over the past 30 years. But with the exception of the Clinton administration's family-leave legislation, Washington has mainly watched from the sidelines as women have struggled to square the demands of child rearing with those of work. America remains the only significant developed nation that has no national child-care policy.

6   Because of that, and because of education and research, women have increasingly come to understand something about having kids: it is demanding work, best done from a bedrock of maturity and security and not to be entered into casually. Many are waiting longer to take it on. Someone once told me I would feel differently about abortion after I had children myself. She was right. I now feel that mothering is so critical and so challenging that to force anyone into its service is immoral.

7   American women know more about their bodies today. They understand the fine points of reproduction; they know what the fetus is and, as important, what it isn't. They have developed a sense of themselves as educated consumers, whether in childbirth, in menopause or in maintenance; they have a sense of ownership of the equipment. They are abetted in this by the increased number of female doctors, who now number almost 50 percent. In their political efforts they can also count female politicians as allies. When *Roe* was handed down, there were no women in the Senate. Today there are 14 female senators. Nine are wholehearted supporters of abortion rights, and three support the right to an abortion with some reservations.

8   Millions of American women have had safe and legal abortions, and can testify to their friends, their daughters and their legislators that it was the right choice at a difficult time. But the abortion rate has slowly fallen. In 2000 it was at its lowest ebb since 1974. Some of that may be because the number of providers has decreased after decades of persistent, sometimes lethal, harassment by anti-abortion forces. But the Centers for Disease Control and Prevention also posit that the decline has something to do with a decrease in unintended pregnancies and increased use of contraception. And of those abortions that did occur, nearly nine out of 10 took place early, in the first trimester.

9   In the first six months after RU-486 was approved in this country, 6 percent of all pregnancies were ended at home with pills rather than in a clinic with surgical intervention, according to a recent report by the Alan Guttmacher Institute. In France, Scotland and Sweden, more than half of early abortions now take place that way. "Medical termination is the wave of the future," says Dr. Paul Blumenthal of Johns Hopkins University, "because it offers control and authority to women who have become accustomed to both."

10   The most powerful predictor of the fate of abortion in this country is not a 30-year-old legal opinion. It is contained in the sum total of these changes in the lives of American women. Taken together, they indubitably argue for a future with more, not less, control over fertility. On this anniversary there is increasing fear that Republican appointments to the court will mean *Roe* will be overturned. Whether the answer to that would be a regimen of pills or a state-by-state political donnybrook is unclear. What is manifest is that those who oppose the right to individual control over the womb lost the battle, not 30 years ago, but day after day after that. The lives of women have changed. We know our rights and our limitations, what we can manage and what we cannot. And sometimes, sadly, that means, and will continue to mean, the end of a pregnancy. This is not 1973. The clock cannot move backward.

Understanding Meaning

1. What momentous court case was decided in 1973? Why was it so important?
2. Quindlen makes the point that while polls have not changed much in thirty years, "everything has changed in the lives of American women. Those changes will set the stage for abortion politics in the years to come, at least as—perhaps more than—the decades-old decision of the high court." Explain what that statement means.
3. What does Quindlen say that she learned from having children? Did that make her less sympathetic towards women who have an abortion?
4. According to Quindlen, in what ways are women better educated today than when *Roe v. Wade* changed the law? In what ways is more support available to them?
5. Why does Quindlen speculate the abortion rate has fallen since 1974?
6. What does she predict about the future of the abortion debate?
7. *CRITICAL THINKING.* How often these days do you hear a young woman say that her goal is to be a stay-at-home mom? Is there a stigma attached to *not* wanting to pursue a career?

Evaluating Strategy

1. Why do you think Quindlen chose to begin her essay as she did?
2. How would you describe the organizational pattern of the essay?
3. What one or two sentences best sum up her thesis?
4. How does she effectively link the conclusion and the introduction?

Appreciating Language

1. Explain the significance of the title.
2. Quindlen is making a very important statement when she writes that American women today know more about their bodies, including "what the fetus is and, as important, what it isn't." Why is that an important statement?
3. What does she mean by the statement: "The impulse to combine the world at home with the world of work is not an opinion today; it is a given"? Do you agree?
4. Do you feel that Quindlen is too extreme when she says that to force anyone into motherhood is immoral? Keep in mind, of course, that Quindlen's opponents generally find abortion immoral.

Writing Suggestions

1. *COLLABORATIVE WRITING.* Go to the library and examine popular magazines from 1973. Look at those designed for the average reader, such as *Time* or *Newsweek*, or women's magazines, such as *Redbook, Ladies Home Journal,* or *Seventeen*. Bring the magazine or your notes to your class. In a small group, write down some conclusions you can draw about women's lives at that time from looking at the advertisements, the photographs, and the titles and subject matter of the articles.
2. Use your group's list as a starting point to write an essay about what women's lives were like at the time of *Roe v. Wade*.
3. Write an essay in which you either agree or disagree with Quindlen's opinion that for most women today, not working outside the home is not an option.
4. Write an essay in which you explain whether you agree with Quindlen about the profound effect that the right to a legal abortion has had on women's lives.

ROBERT RECTOR

Robert Rector received a BA from the College of William and Mary and an MA in political science from Johns Hopkins University. He has published articles in the National Review, The World and I, Human Events, *the* Wall Street Journal, *and the* Los Angeles Times. *His book* America's Failed $5.4 Trillion War on Poverty *is a critical study of the welfare system. Rector is currently a Research Fellow in Domestic Policy Studies at the Heritage Foundation.*

Breaking the Welfare Cycle

CONTEXT: *The following article appeared in the* National Review *in 1997. Although massive welfare reform on a federal level was less than a year old at this point, a similar approach had been practiced in the state of Wisconsin for more than a decade. Rector praises the welfare-to-work program instituted by Governor Tommy Thompson. The overall welfare rolls were trimmed as recipients were encouraged to look for work or perform community service for their benefits.*

1   The first historic battle in the war against the welfare state has been fought and won. The field of battle was Wisconsin, where Gov. Tommy Thompson's reforms have shattered a fifty-year legacy of dependency, and have left welfare apologists fleeing in disarray. Still, a single victory does not mean the war is won—and back in Washington, DC, and in state capitals around the nation, the hosts of high liberalism are girding for their counterattack.

2   Since taking office a decade ago, Gov. Thompson has waged an unremitting campaign against dependency and welfare bloat. The result: a 55 percent drop in Wisconsin's Aid to Families with Dependent Children caseload. In inner-city Milwaukee, the welfare caseload has dropped by a third. Throughout much of the state, AFDC has been all but eliminated: in 28 of Wisconsin's 77 counties, the welfare caseload has shrunk by 80 percent or more.

3   The story gets even better. Generally, as welfare rolls shrink, the most employable people exit first, leaving behind a core of more heavily dependent recipients. Thus, conventional wisdom would expect the decline of Wisconsin's caseload to slow and then halt. Exactly the opposite has happened. As Thompson implemented more rigorous reforms over the last

two years, the pace of dependency reduction accelerated dramatically. Currently the AFDC rolls are plummeting downward by 2 percent per month in Milwaukee and 4 percent in the rest of the state. Overall, the caseload has dropped by almost one-third in the last year alone.

4   Meanwhile, . . . during much of the relevant period national caseloads were soaring. Although in the last two years the national AFDC caseload has fallen by 17 percent, this represents only a peeling back of the explosive growth of dependency which occurred in the early nineties, when AFDC nationwide rocketed up 35 percent. In the majority of states, AFDC dependency remains higher today than when Ronald Reagan left the White House.

5   The lessons to be learned from Wisconsin are of enormous importance. Thompson's reforms are based on three policy principles: (1) reducing unnecessary new entries into AFDC; (2) establishing real work requirements; and (3) erecting incentives to ensure faithful implementation of reform by the bureaucracy.

6   In developing his first principle, Thompson has rediscovered one of the key ideas of traditional charity: a rational system for offering assistance must have a gate-keeping mechanism that separates those who truly need aid from the much larger number of those who do not. Recognizing that the surest way to break the habit of dependency was to prevent it from being formed in the first place, Wisconsin's reform team established a new program, Self-Sufficiency First, with the goal of dissuading unnecessary new entries into AFDC. Self-Sufficiency First provides counseling to new welfare applicants on the negative effects of dependency. It offers short-term aid (such as money for auto repairs) which may help to eliminate the person's need to receive AFDC, and it requires applicants to complete several weeks of supervised job search before their first welfare check is issued. Finally, applicants are warned that they will be required to work in exchange for benefits within a few weeks after entry into the AFDC program. The results are clear: since the implementation of SSF, the number of new AFDC enrollments has been cut nearly in half.

7   The second reform principle is to require recipients to work. The initial step was a realization that government-run job training has a long unsuccessful history, neither reducing dependency nor raising the earning capacity of trainees. For example, a recent Labor Department study of the government's largest training program, the Job Training Partnership Act, finds that JTPA increased the hourly wage rates of female trainees by 3.4 percent and of males not at all.

8   Thus Thompson's staff de-emphasized classroom training and stressed activities leading to immediate employment. Furthermore, if applicants have not obtained a private-sector job after some six weeks of continuous

supervised job search, they are then required to perform community-service work in exchange for ongoing AFDC benefits.

9   Here, as always, the key is in the details. In a typical state, AFDC recipients may theoretically be required to perform community-service work but will receive only a financial slap on the wrist if the work is not done. In Wisconsin, all AFDC recipients are subject to a Pay for Performance rule. If they fail to perform the specified number of hours of work or other activity, their AFDC and Food Stamps benefits are reduced pro rata. Thus, if the recipient is required to perform 30 hours of work but completes only 15, welfare benefits are cut in half. Pay for Performance has eliminated the option of a free income from welfare, making Wisconsin the first state that seriously requires AFDC recipients to earn their welfare checks.

10   Once welfare benefits must be earned, the attractiveness, or economic "utility," of welfare shrivels up and the number entering or remaining on AFDC shrinks dramatically. This lesson is critical. Until now, much of the political debate about reform has envisioned creating millions of make-work jobs for welfare recipients. But the Wisconsin example shows that while mandatory community-service work drives down the caseload, relatively few recipients will actually end up in community-service positions. Instead, the prospect of being forced to do community-service work reduces new welfare enrollments and propels current recipients quickly into private-sector employment.

11   Finally, Thompson realized that the best-designed reforms could be rendered impotent by a hostile or indifferent welfare bureaucracy. Thus he created powerful incentives to guide and motivate the state's welfare establishment. County welfare offices have been forced to earn day-care and training funds by increasing the number of recipients placed in community service or private-sector employment. Moreover, welfare offices that fail to reduce caseloads dramatically face an unprecedented penalty: they can be replaced by outside contractors. Wisconsin's bureaucracy has responded well, implementing reform with unusual efficiency and zeal.

12   In radically reducing Wisconsin's welfare caseload, Gov. Thompson has demolished most of the myths buttressing the liberal welfare state. These include: welfare recipients want to work but no jobs are available; shortages of day care and transportation make work impossible; education and training are the key to cutting dependency; and sharp reductions in welfare caseload will lead to severe economic deprivation.

13   Desperate to find some pretext for dismissing Wisconsin's victory over dependency, liberals claim the drop in caseload is due to a "hot" economy. This is ridiculous; the most robust state economy has never had a fraction of this impact on AFDC dependency. Moreover, if Wisconsin is compared to

various states with lower levels of unemployment, one finds that none of the others have had a large drop in dependency. Another liberal ploy is to claim that Thompson's reforms have raised total welfare costs. This is simply untrue. During Thompson's tenure, aggregate welfare spending on AFDC benefits, administration, day care, and training has fallen some 15 percent in nominal dollars, even as this figure was nearly doubling in the rest of the nation. Adjusted for inflation, Wisconsin's total costs have fallen by more than a third.

14   The most interesting feature of the Wisconsin story is the extraordinary impact of relatively mundane policies. Pay for Performance and Self-Sufficiency First are just common sense, rigorously applied. Any state could implement these policies tomorrow. They are easy to defend politically, as well. Only 2 of Wisconsin's 77 counties currently have time limits; recipients are not booted into the street when their time runs out. True, a significant number of recipients have had all welfare benefits terminated when they failed to work in a community-service position provided by the state. However, when liberals begin to whine about these people, the response is that their checks will be resumed whenever they bother to show up at their job site and begin working. Even the most nimble-tongued apologist has a hard time depicting this as unreasonable and mean.

15   After Thompson's success story, other states must be stampeding to adopt the Wisconsin model, right? Guess again. The main problem at the state level is lack of conservative welfare expertise. The details of reform in most states are left to professional welfare bureaucrats, who are unsympathetic to genuine conservative initiatives and adept at sprucing up variants of the status quo with conservative rhetoric.

16   While sluggishness in state capitals will certainly slow the spread of Wisconsin-style welfare reform, a far more dramatic threat has now emerged from the "End Welfare as We Know It" Clinton White House. Last week the Administration suddenly "discovered" that the Fair Labor Standards Act should apply to AFDC workfare, a rule never intended by Congress and never imposed in the past. Under this ruling, AFDC recipients performing community-service work must be compensated at least at the minimum-wage rate. Of course, guaranteeing all welfare recipients a minimum-wage salary is a bad idea in the first place. Worse, following the normal rules of Clinton-speak, "minimum wage" does not actually mean "minimum wage." The way the Administration's proposed regulations are phrased, the number of hours an AFDC recipient may be required to perform community service cannot exceed his welfare benefits divided by the minimum-wage rate ($4.75 per hour). However, for the Administration, welfare benefits mean only AFDC—other assistance, such as Food Stamps, Medicaid, and public housing, will not be counted.

17   Since the AFDC cash grant is only a small portion of the welfare given to AFDC families, the net effect of Clinton's scheme is to restrict greatly the number of hours a recipient may be required to work. In a few states with very high AFDC benefits the effect would not be too severe. But in the average state, recipients could be forced to work no more than 15 to 20 hours per week. In half the states the number of hours of required work would be lower than that, falling to as little as 5 hours per week. And the effective wage rate (benefits received from all welfare programs divided by hours worked) would be nowhere near $4.75. It would average about $13 per hour and in many cases would exceed $25. The deliberate intent of this policy is to cripple mandatory community-service work, which, as we have seen, is the motor that drives dependency reduction. It is a blatant effort to preserve the status quo by banning successful reform.

18   President Clinton's hypocritical maneuver should surprise no one. For decades liberals have fought relentlessly to prohibit all effective work programs. Indeed, twenty years ago another welfare "reformer," Jimmy Carter, expelled Utah from the AFDC program for, you guessed it, making recipients work for benefits. Despite elaborate obfuscation, not much has changed since.

19   If Mr. Clinton has his way, serious workfare will be emasculated, and Wisconsin's example, like Utah's before it, will be largely forgotten. Within a few years the liberal establishment will return to its mantra: broad economic factors make vast welfare caseloads inevitable; it may be possible to cut dependency at the margin, but only if we are willing to make bold investments in new programs, and so on.

20   The good news is that Congress can easily overturn Mr. Clinton's proposed regulations through new legislation, preferably attached to the overall budget act. But whether the current timid Congress will have the will to do this remains in doubt.

21   Meanwhile, back in Wisconsin, the AFDC caseload continues to drop by 3 percent per month. If Wisconsin's polices are ever adopted by the rest of the nation, taxpayers and recipients will both be huge winners—for dependency is good for neither.

Understanding Meaning

1.   What was done in Wisconsin that makes Rector declare that state's handling of welfare reform a win in the first battle against the welfare state?
2.   Exactly how dramatic has been the change in the welfare system under the leadership of Governor Tommy Thompson?

3. What three lessons, according to Rector, are to be learned from Wisconsin's welfare reform?
4. What does Rector mean when he calls for "real work requirements"? What happens if an individual can't find a job?
5. What threat does Rector state Wisconsin faces because of the decision that the Fair Labor Standards Act should apply to AFDC workfare?
6. *CRITICAL THINKING.* Is there good reason for welfare recipients to work, even if only five hours per week?

Evaluating Strategy

1. What support does Rector use to convince his readers? Do you find it convincing? What objections, if any, could you raise to what he says?
2. How would you describe the essay's organizational plan? How does Rector signal shifts in focus as he moves from one paragraph to another?
3. How effective is the conclusion?

Appreciating Language

1. Would you consider Rector's language subjective or objective? Is the author trying to appeal to his audience's emotions or to their reason? Does that change in the course of the essay? Explain.
2. How effective is the battle imagery of the opening paragraph?
3. Is the author's word choice appropriate for an audience of general readers who are not experts in the field of welfare and welfare reform?

Writing Suggestions

1. Rector boasts that huge numbers of people have been dropped from the welfare rolls in Wisconsin. Does that necessarily mean that they no longer need governmental support, or does it mean they are no longer getting it? Write a short essay explaining how the success of welfare reform should be measured.
2. *COLLABORATIVE WRITING.* Discuss Rector's essay with a group of other students. Ask each member to respond to the following question. What should the goal of public support be: to provide services and assistance the poor need to survive or to provide the means for people to get jobs? Record statements of the group, organizing responses using comparison or classification.

ROBERT REICH

Robert B. Reich (1946–) is University Professor in the Heller Graduate School at Brandeis University. He is the author of numerous books on economics, including The Next American Frontier *(1983) and* The Work of Nations *(1991). A former Rhodes Scholar at Oxford, Reich is a popular lecturer and frequent guest on television talk shows. He served as secretary of labor in the first Clinton administration.*

Why the Rich are Getting Richer and the Poor, Poorer

CONTEXT: *In the following chapter from* The Work of Nations, *Reich shows how the composition of the American labor force has changed in recent decades. Since the 1970s, traditional industrial workers have been replaced by machines and by cheaper foreign labor. Displaced workers from this sector of the economy have moved into the already crowded market of service workers, who are themselves being rapidly replaced by automation. Only those persons who deal in "symbolic analysis" (words and ideas) are markedly improving their lot in life. (They include publicists, engineers, marketing experts, and various kinds of consultants.) Because of these three different labor markets, it becomes increasingly difficult to make generalizations about the health of the American economy.*

[T]he division of labour is limited by the extent of the market.

ADAM SMITH, *An Inquiry into the Nature and Causes of the Wealth of Nations (1776)*

1   Regardless of how your job is officially classified (manufacturing, service, managerial, technical, secretarial, and so on), or the industry in which you work (automotive, steel, computer, advertising, finance, food processing), your real competitive position in the world economy is coming to depend on the function you perform in it. Herein lies the basic reason why incomes are diverging. The fortunes of routine producers are declining. In-person servers are also becoming poorer, although their fates are less clear-cut. But symbolic analysts—who solve, identify, and broker new problems—are, by and large, succeeding in the world economy.

2   All Americans used to be in roughly the same economic boat. Most rose or fell together, as the corporations in which they were employed, the industries comprising such corporations, and the national economy as a whole became more productive—or languished. But national borders no longer define our economic fates. We are now in different boats, one sinking rapidly, one sinking more slowly, and the third rising steadily.

2

3   The boat containing routine producers is sinking rapidly. Recall that by midcentury routine production workers in the United States were paid relatively well. The giant pyramidlike organizations at the core of each major industry coordinated their prices and investments—avoiding the harsh winds of competition and thus maintaining healthy earnings. Some of these earnings, in turn, were reinvested in new plant and equipment (yielding ever-larger-scale economies); another portion went to top managers and investors. But a large and increasing portion went to middle managers and production workers. Work stoppages posed such a threat to high-volume production that organized labor was able to exact an ever-larger premium for its cooperation. And the pattern of wages established within the core corporations influenced the pattern throughout the national economy. Thus the growth of a relatively affluent middle class, able to purchase all the wondrous things produced in high volume by the core corporations.

4   But, as has been observed, the core is rapidly breaking down into global webs which earn their largest profits from clever problem-solving, -identifying, and brokering. As the costs of transporting standard things and of communicating information about them continue to drop, profit margins on high-volume, standardized production are thinning, because there are few barriers to entry. Modern factories and state-of-the-art machinery can be installed almost anywhere on the globe. Routine producers in the United States, then, are in direct competition with millions of routine producers in other nations. Twelve thousand people are added to the world's population every hour, most of whom, eventually, will happily work for a small fraction of the wages of routine producers in America.[1]

5   The consequence is clearest in older, heavy industries, where high-volume, standardized production continues its ineluctable move to where labor is cheapest and most accessible around the world. Thus, for example, the Maquiladora factories cluttered along the Mexican side of the U.S. border in the sprawling shanty towns of Tijuana, Mexicali, Nogales, Agua Prieta, and Ciudad Juárez—factories owned mostly by Americans, but increasingly by

---

[1] The reader should note, of course, that lower wages in other areas of the world are of no particular attraction to global capital unless workers there are sufficiently productive to make the labor cost of producing *each unit* lower there than in higher-wage regions. Productivity in many low-wage areas of the world has improved due to the ease with which state-of-the-art factories and equipment can be installed there.

Japanese—in which more than a half million routine producers assemble parts into finished goods to be shipped into the United States.

6   The same story is unfolding worldwide. Until the late 1970s, AT&T had depended on routine producers in Shreveport, Louisiana, to assemble standard telephones. It then discovered that routine producers in Singapore would perform the same tasks at a far lower cost. Facing intense competition from other global webs, AT&T's strategic brokers felt compelled to switch. So in the early 1980s they stopped hiring routine producers in Shreveport and began hiring cheaper routine producers in Singapore. But under this kind of pressure for ever lower high-volume production costs, today's Singaporean can easily end up as yesterday's Louisianan. By the late 1980s, AT&T's strategic brokers found that routine producers in Thailand were eager to assemble telephones for a small fraction of the wages of routine producers in Singapore. Thus, in 1989, AT&T stopped hiring Singaporeans to make telephones and began hiring even cheaper routine producers in Thailand.

7   The search for ever lower wages has not been confined to heavy industry. Routine data processing is equally footloose. Keypunch operators located anywhere around the world can enter data into computers, linked by satellite or transoceanic fiber-optic cable, and take it out again. As the rates charged by satellite networks continue to drop, and as more satellites and fiber-optic cables become available (reducing communication costs still further), routine data processors in the United States find themselves in ever more direct competition with their counterparts abroad, who are often eager to work for far less.

8   By 1990, keypunch operators in the United States were earning, at most, $6.50 per hour. But keypunch operators throughout the rest of the world were willing to work for a fraction of this. Thus, many potential American data-processing jobs were disappearing, and the wages and benefits of the remaining ones were in decline. Typical was Saztec International, a $20-million-a-year data-processing firm headquartered in Kansas City, whose American strategic brokers contracted with routine data processors in Manila and with American-owned firms that needed such data-processing services. Compared with the average Philippine income of $1,700 per year, data-entry operators working for Saztec earn the princely sum of $2,650. The remainder of Saztec's employees were American problem-solvers and -identifiers, searching for ways to improve the worldwide system and find new uses to which it could be put.[2]

---

[2] John Maxwell Hamilton, "A Bit Player Buys Into the Computer Age," *The New York Times Business World*, December 3, 1989, p. 14.

9   By 1990, American Airlines was employing over 1,000 data processors in Barbados and the Dominican Republic to enter names and flight numbers from used airline tickets (flown daily to Barbados from airports around the United States) into a giant computer bank located in Dallas. Chicago publisher R. R. Donnelley was sending entire manuscripts to Barbados for entry into computers in preparation for printing. The New York Life Insurance Company was dispatching insurance claims to Castleisland, Ireland, where routine producers, guided by simple directions, entered the claims and determined the amounts due, then instantly transmitted the computations back to the United States. (When the firm advertised in Ireland for twenty-five data-processing jobs, it received six hundred applications.) And McGraw-Hill was processing subscription renewal and marketing information for its magazines in nearby Galway. Indeed, literally millions of routine workers around the world were receiving information, converting it into computer-readable form, and then sending it back—at the speed of electronic impulses—whence it came.

10   The simple coding of computer software has also entered into world commerce. India, with a large English-speaking population of technicians happy to do routine programming cheaply, is proving to be particularly attractive to global webs in need of this service. By 1990, Texas Instruments maintained a software development facility in Bangalore, linking fifty Indian programmers by satellite to TI's Dallas headquarters. Spurred by this and similar ventures, the Indian government was building a teleport in Poona, intended to make it easier and less expensive for many other firms to send their routine software design specifications for coding.[3]

3

11   This shift of routine production jobs from advanced to developing nations is a great boon to many workers in such nations who otherwise would be jobless or working for much lower wages. These workers, in turn, now have more money with which to purchase symbolic-analytic services from advanced nations (often embedded within all sorts of complex products).

---

[3] Udayan Gupta, "U.S.-India Satellite Link Stands to Cut Software Costs," *The Wall Street Journal*, March 6, 1989, p. B2.

The trend is also beneficial to everyone around the world who can now obtain high-volume, standardized products (including information and software) more cheaply than before.

12   But these benefits do not come without certain costs. In particular the burden is borne by those who no longer have good-paying routine production jobs within advanced economies like the United States. Many of these people used to belong to unions or at least benefited from prevailing wage rates established in collective bargaining agreements. But as the old corporate bureaucracies have flattened into global webs, bargaining leverage has been lost. Indeed, the tacit national bargain is no more.

13   Despite the growth in the number of new jobs in the United States, union membership has withered. In 1960, 35 percent of all nonagricultural workers in America belonged to a union. But by 1980 that portion had fallen to just under a quarter, and by 1989 to about 17 percent. Excluding government employees, union membership was down to 13.4 percent.[4] This was a smaller proportion even than in the early 1930s, before the National Labor Relations Act created a legally protected right to labor representation. The drop in membership has been accompanied by a growing number of collective bargaining agreements to freeze wages at current levels, reduce wage levels of entering workers, or reduce wages overall. This is an important reason why the long economic recovery that began in 1982 produced a smaller rise in unit labor costs than any of the eight recoveries since World War II—the low rate of unemployment during its course notwithstanding.

14   Routine production jobs have vanished fastest in traditional unionized industries (autos, steel, and rubber, for example), where average wages have kept up with inflation. This is because the jobs of older workers in such industries are protected by seniority; the youngest workers are the first to be laid off. Faced with a choice of cutting wages or cutting the number of jobs, a majority of union members (secure in the knowledge that there are many who are junior to them who will be laid off first) often have voted for the latter.

15   Thus the decline in union membership has been most striking among young men entering the work force without a college education. In the early 1950s, more than 40 percent of this group joined unions; by the late 1980s, less than 20 percent (if public employees are excluded, less than

---

[4] *Statistical Abstract of the United States* (Washington, D.C.: U.S. Government Printing Office, 1989), p. 416, Table 684.

10 percent).[5] In steelmaking, for example, although many older workers remained employed, almost half of all routine steelmaking jobs in America vanished between 1974 and 1988 (from 480,000 to 260,000). Similarly with automobiles: During the 1980s, the United Auto Workers lost 500,000 members—one-third of their total at the start of the decade. General Motors alone cut 150,000 American production jobs during the 1980s (even as it added employment abroad). Another consequence of the same phenomenon: The gap between the average wages of unionized and nonunionized workers widened dramatically—from 14.6 percent in 1973 to 20.4 percent by the end of the 1980s.[6] The lesson is clear. If you drop out of high school or have no more than a high school diploma, do not expect a good routine production job to be awaiting you.

16   Also vanishing are lower- and middle-level management jobs involving routine production. Between 1981 and 1986, more than 780,000 foremen, supervisors, and section chiefs lost their jobs through plant closings and layoffs.[7] Large numbers of assistant division heads, assistant directors, assistant managers, and vice presidents also found themselves jobless. GM shed more than 40,000 white-collar employees and planned to eliminate another 25,000 by the mid-1990s.[8] As America's core pyramids metamorphosed into global webs, many middle-level routine producers were as obsolete as routine workers on the line.

17   As has been noted, foreign-owned webs are hiring some Americans to do routine production in the United States. Philips, Sony, and Toyota factories are popping up all over—to the self-congratulatory applause of the nation's governors and mayors, who have lured them with promises of tax abatements and new sewers, among other amenities. But as these ebullient politicians will soon discover, the foreign-owned factories are highly automated and will become far more so in years to come. Routine production jobs account for a small fraction of the cost of producing most items in the United States and other advanced nations, and this fraction will continue to decline sharply as computer-integrated robots take over. In 1977 it took routine producers thirty-five hours to assemble an automobile in the United States; it is estimated that by the

---

[5] Calculations from Current Population Surveys by L. Katz and A. Revenga, "Changes in the Structure of Wages: U.S. and Japan," National Bureau of Economic Research, September 1989.

[6] U.S. Department of Commerce, Bureau of Labor Statistics, "Wages of Unionized and Non-Unionized Workers," various issues.

[7] U.S. Department of Labor, Bureau of Labor Statistics, "Reemployment Increases Among Displaced Workers," *BLS News*, USDL 86-414, October 14, 1986, Table 6.

[8] *The Wall Street Journal*, February 16, 1990, p. A5.

mid-1990s, Japanese-owned factories in America will be producing finished automobiles using only eight hours of a routine producer's time.[9]

18   The productivity and resulting wages of American workers who run such robotic machinery may be relatively high, but there may not be many such jobs to go around. A case in point: In the late 1980s, Nippon Steel joined with America's ailing Inland Steel to build a new $400 million cold-rolling mill fifty miles west of Gary, Indiana. The mill was celebrated for its state-of-the-art technology, which cut the time to produce a coil of steel from twelve days to about one hour. In fact, the entire plant could be run by a small team of technicians, which became clear when Inland subsequently closed two of its old cold-rolling mills, laying off hundreds of routine workers. Governors and mayors take note: Your much-ballyhooed foreign factories may end up employing distressingly few of your constituents.

19   Overall, the decline in routine jobs has hurt men more than women. This is because the routine production jobs held by men in high-volume metal-bending manufacturing industries had paid higher wages than the routine production jobs held by women in textiles and data processing. As both sets of jobs have been lost, American women in routine production have gained more equal footing with American men—equally poor footing, that is. This is a major reason why the gender gap between male and female wages began to close during the 1980s.

4

20   The second of the three boats, carrying in-person servers, is sinking as well, but somewhat more slowly and unevenly. Most in-person servers are paid at or just slightly above the minimum wage and many work only part-time, with the result that their take-home pay is modest, to say the least. Nor do they typically receive all the benefits (health care, life insurance, disability, and so forth) garnered by routine producers in large manufacturing corporations or by symbolic analysts affiliated with the more affluent threads of global webs.[10] In-person servers are sheltered from the direct effects of

---

[9] Figures from the International Motor Vehicles Program, Massachusetts Institute of Technology, 1989.

[10] The growing portion of the American labor force engaged in in-person services, relative to routine production, thus helps explain why the number of Americans lacking health insurance increased by at least 6 million during the 1980s.

global competition and, like everyone else, benefit from access to lower-cost products from around the world. But they are not immune to its indirect effects.

21   For one thing, in-person servers increasingly compete with former routine production workers, who, no longer able to find well-paying routine production jobs, have few alternatives but to seek in-person service jobs. The Bureau of Labor Statistics estimates that of the 2.8 million manufacturing workers who lost their jobs during the early 1980s, fully one-third were rehired in service jobs paying at least 20 percent less.[11] In-person servers must also compete with high school graduates and dropouts who years before had moved easily into routine production jobs but no longer can. And if demographic predictions about the American work force in the first decades of the twenty-first century are correct (and they are likely to be, since most of the people who will comprise the work force are already identifiable), most new entrants into the job market will be black or Hispanic men, or women—groups that in years past have possessed relatively weak technical skills. This will result in an even larger number of people crowding into in-person services. Finally, in-person servers will be competing with growing numbers of immigrants, both legal and illegal, for whom in-person services will comprise the most accessible jobs. (It is estimated that between the mid-1980s and the end of the century, about a quarter of all workers entering the American labor force will be immigrants.[12])

22   Perhaps the fiercest competition that in-person servers face comes from labor-saving machinery (much of it invented, designed, fabricated, or assembled in other nations, of course). Automated tellers, computerized cashiers, automatic car washes, robotized vending machines, self-service gasoline pumps, and all similar gadgets substitute for the human beings that customers once encountered. Even telephone operators are fast disappearing, as electronic sensors and voice simulators become capable of carrying on conversations that are reasonably intelligent, and always polite. Retail sales workers—among the largest groups of in-person servers—are similarly imperiled. Through personal computers linked to television screens, tomorrow's consumers will be able to buy furniture, appliances, and all sorts of electronic toys from their living rooms—examining the

[11] U.S. Department of Labor, Bureau of Labor Statistics, "Reemployment Increases Among Displaced Workers," October 14, 1986.

[12] Federal Immigration and Naturalization Service, *Statistical Yearbook* (Washington, D.C.: U.S. Government Printing Office, 1986, 1987).

merchandise from all angles, selecting whatever color, size, special features, and price seem most appealing, and then transmitting the order instantly to warehouses from which the selections will be shipped directly to their homes. So, too, with financial transactions, airline and hotel reservations, rental car agreements, and similar contracts, which will be executed between consumers in their homes and computer banks somewhere else on the globe.[13]

23   Advanced economies like the United States will continue to generate sizable numbers of new in-person service jobs, of course, the automation of older ones notwithstanding. For every bank teller who loses her job to an automated teller, three new jobs open for aerobics instructors. Human beings, it seems, have an almost insatiable desire for personal attention. But the intense competition nevertheless ensures that the wages of in-person servers will remain relatively low. In-person servers—working on their own, or else dispersed widely amid many small establishments, filling all sorts of personal-care niches—cannot readily organize themselves into labor unions or create powerful lobbies to limit the impact of such competition.

24   In two respects, demographics will work in favor of in-person servers, buoying their collective boat slightly. First, as has been noted, the rate of growth of the American work force is slowing. In particular, the number of younger workers is shrinking. Between 1985 and 1995, the number of eighteen- to twenty-four-year-olds will have declined by 17.5 percent. Thus, employers will have more incentive to hire and train in-person servers whom they might previously have avoided. But this demographic relief from the competitive pressures will be only temporary. The cumulative procreative energies of the postwar baby-boomers (born between 1946 and 1964) will result in a new surge of workers by 2010 or thereabouts.[14] And immigration—both legal and illegal—shows every sign of increasing in years to come.

25   Next, by the second decade of the twenty-first century, the number of Americans aged sixty-five and over will be rising precipitously, as the baby-boomers reach retirement age and live longer. Their life expectancies will lengthen not just because fewer of them will have smoked their way to their graves and more will have eaten better than their parents, but also because

---

[13] See Claudia H. Deutsch, "The Powerful Push for Self-Service," *The New York Times*, April 9, 1989, section 3, p. 1.

[14] U.S. Bureau of the Census, Current Population Reports, Series P-23, No. 138, Tables 2-1, 4-6. See W. Johnson, A. Packer, et al., *Workforce 2000: Work and Workers for the 21st Century* (Indianapolis: Hudson Institute, 1987).

they will receive all sorts of expensive drugs and therapies designed to keep them alive—barely. By 2035, twice as many Americans will be elderly as in 1988, and the number of octogenarians is expected to triple. As these decaying baby-boomers ingest all the chemicals and receive all the treatments, they will need a great deal of personal attention. Millions of deteriorating bodies will require nurses, nursing-home operators, hospital administrators, orderlies, home-care providers, hospice aides, and technicians to operate and maintain all the expensive machinery that will monitor and temporarily stave off final disintegration. There might even be a booming market for euthanasia specialists. In-person servers catering to the old and ailing will be in strong demand.[15]

26   One small problem: The decaying baby-boomers will not have enough money to pay for these services. They will have used up their personal savings years before. Their Social Security payments will, of course, have been used by the government to pay for the previous generation's retirement and to finance much of the budget deficits of the 1980s. Moreover, with relatively fewer young Americans in the population, the supply of housing will likely exceed the demand, with the result that the boomers' major investments— their homes—will be worth less (in inflation-adjusted dollars) when they retire than they planned for. In consequence, the huge cost of caring for the graying boomers will fall on many of the same people who will be paid to care for them. It will be like a great sump pump: In-person servers of the twenty-first century will have an abundance of health-care jobs, but a large portion of their earnings will be devoted to Social Security payments and income taxes, which will in turn be used to pay their salaries. The net result: no real improvement in their standard of living.

27   The standard of living of in-person servers also depends, indirectly, on the standard of living of the Americans they serve who are engaged in world commerce. To the extent that *these* Americans are richly rewarded by the rest of the world for what they contribute, they will have more money to lavish upon in-person services. Here we find the only form of "trickle-down" economics that has a basis in reality. A waitress in a town whose major factory has just been closed is unlikely to earn a high wage or enjoy much job security; in a swank resort populated by film producers and banking moguls, she is apt to do reasonably well. So, too, with nations. In-person servers in Bangladesh may spend their days performing roughly the same tasks as

---

[15] The Census Bureau estimates that by the year 2000, at least 12 million Americans will work in health services—well over 6 percent of the total work force.

in-person servers in the United States, but have a far lower standard of living for their efforts. The difference comes in the value that their customers add to the world economy. I shall return to this issue in a later chapter.

5

28 Unlike the boats of routine producers and in-person servers, however, the vessel containing America's symbolic analysts is rising. Worldwide demand for their insights is growing as the ease and speed of communicating them steadily increases. Not every symbolic analyst is rising as quickly or as dramatically as every other, of course; symbolic analysts at the low end are barely holding their own in the world economy. But symbolic analysts at the top are in such great demand worldwide that they have difficulty keeping track of all their earnings. Never before in history has opulence on such a scale been gained by people who have earned it, and done so legally.

29 Among symbolic analysts in the middle range are American scientists and researchers who are busily selling their discoveries to global enterprise webs. They are not limited to American customers. If the strategic brokers in General Motors' headquarters refuse to pay a high price for a new means of making high-strength ceramic engines dreamed up by a team of engineers affiliated with Carnegie-Mellon University in Pittsburgh, the strategic brokers of Honda or Mercedes-Benz are likely to be more than willing.

30 So, too, with the insights of America's ubiquitous management consultants, which are being sold for large sums to eager entrepreneurs in Europe and Latin America. Also, the insights of America's energy consultants, sold for even larger sums to Arab sheikhs. American design engineers are providing insights to Olivetti, Mazda, Siemens, and other global webs; American marketers, techniques for learning what worldwide consumers will buy; American advertisers, ploys for ensuring that they actually do. American architects are issuing designs and blueprints for opera houses, art galleries, museums, luxury hotels, and residential complexes in the world's major cities; American commercial property developers, marketing these properties to worldwide investors and purchasers.

31 Americans who specialize in the gentle art of public relations are in demand by corporations, governments, and politicians in virtually every nation. So, too, are American political consultants, some of whom, at this writing, are advising the Hungarian Socialist Party, the remnant of Hungary's ruling Communists, on how to salvage a few parliamentary seats in the

nation's first free election in more than forty years. Also at this writing, a team of American agricultural consultants are advising the managers of a Soviet farm collective employing 1,700 Russians eighty miles outside Moscow. As noted, American investment bankers and lawyers specializing in financial circumnavigations are selling their insights to Asians and Europeans who are eager to discover how to make large amounts of money by moving large amounts of money.

32   Developing nations, meanwhile, are hiring American civil engineers to advise on building roads and dams. The present thaw in the Cold War will no doubt expand these opportunities. American engineers from Bechtel (a global firm notable for having employed both Caspar Weinberger and George Shultz for much larger sums than either earned in the Reagan administration) have begun helping the Soviets design and install a new generation of nuclear reactors. Nations also are hiring American bankers and lawyers to help them renegotiate the terms of their loans with global banks, and Washington lobbyists to help them with Congress, the Treasury, the World Bank, the IMF, and other politically sensitive institutions. In fits of obvious desperation, several nations emerging from communism have even hired American economists to teach them about capitalism.

33   Almost everyone around the world is buying the skills and insights of Americans who manipulate oral and visual symbols—musicians, sound engineers, film producers, makeup artists, directors, cinematographers, actors and actresses, boxers, scriptwriters, songwriters, and set designers. Among the wealthiest of symbolic analysts are Steven Spielberg, Bill Cosby, Charles Schulz, Eddie Murphy, Sylvester Stallone, Madonna, and other star directors and performers—who are almost as well known on the streets of Dresden and Tokyo as in the Back Bay of Boston. Less well rewarded but no less renowned are the unctuous anchors on Turner Broadcasting's Cable News, who appear daily, via satellite, in places ranging from Vietnam to Nigeria. Vanna White is the world's most watched game-show hostess. Behind each of these familiar faces is a collection of American problem-solvers, -identifiers, and brokers who train, coach, advise, promote, amplify, direct, groom, represent, and otherwise add value to their talents.[16]

34   There are also the insights of senior American executives who occupy the world headquarters of global "American" corporations and the national

---

[16] In 1989, the entertainment business summoned to the United States $5.5 billion in foreign earnings—making it among the nation's largest export industries, just behind aerospace. U.S. Department of Commerce, International Trade Commission, "Composition of U.S. Exports," various issues.

or regional headquarters of global "foreign" corporations. Their insights are duly exported to the rest of the world through the webs of global enterprise. IBM does not export many machines from the United States, for example. Big Blue makes machines all over the globe and services them on the spot. Its prime American exports are symbolic and analytic. From IBM's world headquarters in Armonk, New York, emanate strategic brokerage and related management services bound for the rest of the world. In return, IBM's top executives are generously rewarded.

6

35   The most important reason for this expanding world market and increasing global demand for the symbolic and analytic insights of Americans has been the dramatic improvement in worldwide communication and transportation technologies. Designs, instructions, advice, and visual and audio symbols can be communicated more and more rapidly around the globe, with ever-greater precision and at ever-lower cost. Madonna's voice can be transported to billions of listeners, with perfect clarity, on digital compact disks. A new invention emanating from engineers in Battelle's laboratory in Columbus, Ohio, can be sent almost anywhere via modem, in a form that will allow others to examine it in three dimensions through enhanced computer graphics. When face-to-face meetings are still required—and videoconferencing will not suffice—it is relatively easy for designers, consultants, advisers, artists, and executives to board supersonic jets and, in a matter of hours, meet directly with their worldwide clients, customers, audiences, and employees.

36   With rising demand comes rising compensation. Whether in the form of licensing fees, fees for service, salaries, or shares in final profits, the economic result is much the same. There are also nonpecuniary rewards. One of the best-kept secrets among symbolic analysts is that so many of them enjoy their work. In fact, much of it does not count as work at all, in the traditional sense. The work of routine producers and in-person servers is typically monotonous; it causes muscles to tire or weaken and involves little independence or discretion. The "work" of symbolic analysts, by contrast, often involves puzzles, experiments, games, a significant amount of chatter, and substantial discretion over what to do next. Few routine producers or in-person servers would "work" if they did not need to earn the money. Many symbolic analysts would "work" even if money were no object.

7

37   At midcentury, when America was a national market dominated by core pyramid-shaped corporations, there were constraints on the earnings of people at the highest rungs. First and most obviously, the market for their services was largely limited to the borders of the nation. In addition, whatever conceptual value they might contribute was small relative to the value gleaned from large scale—and it was dependent on large scale for whatever income it was to summon. Most of the problems to be identified and solved had to do with enhancing the efficiency of production and improving the flow of materials, parts, assembly, and distribution. Inventors searched for the rare breakthrough revealing an entirely new product to be made in high volume; management consultants, executives, and engineers thereafter tried to speed and synchronize its manufacture, to better achieve scale efficiencies; advertisers and marketers sought then to whet the public's appetite for the standard item that emerged. Since white-collar earnings increased with larger scale, there was considerable incentive to expand the firm; indeed, many of America's core corporations grew far larger than scale economies would appear to have justified.

38   By the 1990s, in contrast, the earnings of symbolic analysts were limited neither by the size of the national market nor by the volume of production of the firms with which they were affiliated. The marketplace was worldwide, and conceptual value was high relative to value added from scale efficiencies.

39   There had been another constraint on high earnings, which also gave way by the 1990s. At midcentury, the compensation awarded to top executives and advisers of the largest of America's core corporations could not be grossly out of proportion to that of low-level production workers. It would be unseemly for executives who engaged in highly visible rounds of bargaining with labor unions, and who routinely responded to government requests to moderate prices, to take home wages and benefits wildly in excess of what other Americans earned. Unless white-collar executives restrained themselves, moreover, blue-collar production workers could not be expected to restrain their own demands for higher wages. Unless both groups exercised restraint, the government could not be expected to forbear from imposing direct controls and regulations.

40   At the same time, the wages of production workers could not be allowed to sink too low, lest there be insufficient purchasing power in the economy. After all, who would buy all the goods flowing out of American factories if not American workers? This, too, was part of the tacit bargain struck between American managers and their workers.

41   Recall the oft-repeated corporate platitude of the era about the chief executive's responsibility to carefully weigh and balance the interests of the corporation's disparate stakeholders. Under the stewardship of the corporate statesman, no set of stakeholders—least of all white-collar executives—was to gain a disproportionately large share of the benefits of corporate activity; nor was any stakeholder—especially the average worker—to be left with a share that was disproportionately small. Banal though it was, this idea helped to maintain the legitimacy of the core American corporation in the eyes of most Americans, and to ensure continued economic growth.

42   But by the 1990s, these informal norms were evaporating, just as (and largely because) the core American corporation was vanishing. The links between top executives and the American production worker were fading: An ever-increasing number of subordinates and contractees were foreign, and a steadily growing number of American routine producers were working for foreign-owned firms. An entire cohort of middle-level managers, who had once been deemed "white collar," had disappeared; and, increasingly, American executives were exporting their insights to global enterprise webs.

43   As the American corporation itself became a global web almost indistinguishable from any other, its stakeholders were turning into a large and diffuse group, spread over the world. Such global stakeholders were less visible, and far less noisy, than national stakeholders. And as the American corporation sold its goods and services all over the world, the purchasing power of American workers became far less relevant to its economic survival.

44   Thus have the inhibitions been removed. The salaries and benefits of America's top executives, and many of their advisers and consultants, have soared to what years before would have been unimaginable heights, even as those of other Americans have declined.

Understanding Meaning

1.   What is the main idea that Reich is trying to make about how changes in the way business is done have changed the wages of American workers?
2.   The three groups that he talks about are production workers, in-person servers, and symbolic analysts. How is each of these groups being affected by the fact that more and more work is being done overseas?
3.   What sorts of professions are included in what Reich calls "symbolic analysts"? Why are people in those professions faring better than some others?

4. What are some of the reasons for massive layoffs of production workers? What does that do to the in-person servers?
5. According to Reich, why are not as many in-person servers unionized as factory workers? Why are younger factory workers not as likely to join unions as older ones were?
6. *CRITICAL THINKING.* Speculate about how what Reich says relates to a career that you have been considering. Does what he says affect your life in any other way? Explain.

Evaluating Strategy

1. Explain the boat imagery that is the controlling metaphor of the piece.
2. *BLENDING THE MODES.* Much of Reich's discussion of the economy is abstract. Where do examples make his points clearer?
3. Where does Reich make effective use of statistics to back up his assertions?

Appreciating Language

1. What would you assume about Reich's audience, based on his level of diction?
2. What was your reaction to Reich's use of such terms as *in-person server* and *symbolic analyst?*

Writing Suggestions

1. Describe the attitudes about work and wealth you have heard expressed by friends, neighbors, and other students. Do they feel that opportunities are shrinking? Have any lost their jobs? Are students on your campus hopeful or dubious about their chances of finding good jobs and rewarding careers after graduation? Write a short essay that summarizes the views you often hear expressed.
2. *COLLABORATIVE WRITING.* Discuss this essay in a small group. Do they agree with Reich or have a different opinion? Write a brief essay that summarizes your group's views. If people have differing opinions, consider drafting a comparison pro and con essay or a division paper that outlines a variety of viewpoints.

ARMANDO RENDÓN

Armando Rendón (1939–) was raised in San Antonio, Texas. He is currently vice president of ATM Systems, a Chicago-based counseling firm. He has published articles in the Washington Post *and* Civil Rights Digest. *Rendón also wrote a film script,* El Chicano. *In 1971 he published* Chicano Manifesto, *which outlined his views of the place of Mexicans in American society.*

Kiss of Death

CONTEXT: *In this section from the* Chicano Manifesto, *Rendón argues the importance of Hispanics resisting assimilation into mainstream American society and maintaining their language and culture to avoid "being sucked into the vacuum of the dominant society."*

1   I nearly fell victim to the Anglo. My childhood was spent in the West Side barrio of San Antonio. I lived in my grandmother's house on Ruiz Street just below Zarzamora Creek. I did well in the elementary grades and learned English quickly.

2   Spanish was off-limits in school anyway, and teachers and relatives taught me early that my mother tongue would be of no help in making good grades and becoming a success. Yet Spanish was the language I used in playing and arguing with friends. Spanish was the language I spoke with my *abuelita*, my dear grandmother, as I ate *atole* on those cold mornings when I used to wake at dawn to her clattering dishes in the tiny kitchen; or when I would cringe in mock horror at old folk tales she would tell me late at night.

3   But the lesson took effect anyway. When, at the age of ten, I went with my mother to California, to the San Francisco Bay Area where she found work during the war years, I had my first real opportunity to strip myself completely of my heritage. In California the schools I attended were all Anglo except for this little mexicanito. At least, I never knew anyone who admitted he was Mexican and I certainly never thought to ask. When my name was accented incorrectly, Réndon instead of Rendón, that was all right; finally I must have gotten tired of correcting people or just didn't bother.

4   I remember a summertime visit home a few years after living on the West Coast. At an evening gathering of almost the whole family—uncles, aunts, nephews, nieces, my *abuelita*—we sat outdoors through the dusk

until the dark had fully settled. Then the lights were turned on; someone brought out a Mexican card game, the *Lotería El Diablito*, similar to bingo. But instead of rows of numbers on a pasteboard, there were figures of persons, animals, and objects on cards corresponding to figures set in rows on a pasteboard. We used frijoles (pinto beans) to mark each figure on our card as the leader went through the deck one by one. The word for tree was called: *Arbol!* It completed a row; I had won. Then to check my card I had to name each figure again. When I said the word for tree, it didn't come at all as I wanted it to; AR-BOWL with the accent on the last syllable and sounding like an Anglo tourist. There was some all-around kidding of me and good-natured laughter over the incident, and it passed.

5   But if I had not been speaking much Spanish up until then, I spoke even less afterward. Even when my mother, who speaks both Spanish and English fluently, spoke to me in Spanish, I would respond in English. By the time I graduated from high school and prepared to enter college, the break was nearly complete. Seldom during college did I admit to being a Mexican-American. Only when Latin American students pressed me about my surname did I admit my Spanish descent, or when it proved an asset in meeting coeds from Latin American countries.

6   My ancestry had become a shadow, fainter and fainter about me. I felt no particular allegiance to it, drew no inspiration from it, and elected generally to let it fade away. I clicked with the Anglo mind-set in college, mastered it, you might say. I even became editor of the campus biweekly newspaper as a junior, and editor of the literary magazine as a senior—not bad, now that I look back, for a tortillas-and-beans Chicano upbringing to beat the Anglo at his own game.

7   The point of my "success," of course, was that I had been assimilated; I had bought the white man's world. After getting my diploma I was set to launch out into a career in newspaper reporting and writing. There was no thought in my mind of serving my people, telling their story, or making anything right for anybody but myself. Instead I had dreams of Pulitzer Prizes, syndicated columns, foreign correspondent assignments, front-page stories—that was for me. Then something happened.

8   A Catholic weekly newspaper in Sacramento offered me a position as a reporter and feature writer. I had a job on a Bay Area daily as a copyboy at the time, with the opportunity to become a reporter. But I'd just been married, and there were a number of other reasons to consider: there'd be a variety of assignments, Sacramento was the state capital, it was a good town in which to raise a family, and the other job lacked promise for upward mobility. I decided to take the offer.

9   My wife and I moved to Sacramento in the fall of 1961, and in a few weeks the radicalization of this Chicano began. It wasn't a book I read or a great leader awakening me, for we had no Chávezes or Tijerinas or Gonzálezes at the time; and it was no revelation from above. It was my own people who rescued me. There is a large Chicano population in Sacramento, today one of the most activist in northern California, but at the time factionalized and still dependent on the social and church organizations for identity. But together we found each other.

10   My job soon brought me into contact with many Chicanos as well as with the recently immigrated Mexicans, located in the barrios that Sacramento had allocated to the "Mexicans." I found my people striving to survive in an alien environment among foreign people. One of the stories I covered concerned a phenomenon called Cursillos de Cristiandad (Little Courses in Christianity), intense, three-day group-sensitivity sessions whose chief objective is the re-Christianization of Catholics. To cover the story properly I talked my editor into letting me take a Cursillo.

11   Not only was much revealed to me about the phony gilt lining of religion which I had grown up believing was the Church, but there was an added and highly significant side effect—cultural shock! I rediscovered my own people, or perhaps they redeemed me. Within the social dimension of the Cursillo, for the first time in many years I became reimmersed in a tough, *macho ambiente* (an entirely Mexican male environment). Only Spanish was spoken. The effect was shattering. It was as if my tongue, after being struck dumb as a child, had been loosened.

12   Because we were located in cramped quarters, with limited facilities, and the cooks, lecturers, priests, and participants were men only, the old sense of *machismo* and *camarada* was revived and given new perspective. I was cast in a spiritual setting which was a perfect background for reviving my Chicano soul. Reborn but imperfectly, I still had a lot to learn about myself and my people. But my understanding deepened and renewed itself as the years went by. I visited bracero camps with teams of Chicanos; sometimes with priests taking the sacraments; sometimes only Chicanos, offering advice or assistance with badly needed food and clothing, distributed through a bingo-game technique; and on occasion, music for group singing provided by a phonograph or a guitar. Then there were barrio organization work; migrant worker programs; a rural self-help community development project; and confrontation with antipoverty agencies, with the churches, with government officials, and with cautious Chicanos, too.

13   In a little San Francisco magazine called *Way*, I wrote in a March 1966 article discussing "The Other Mexican-American":

The Mexican-American must answer at the same time: Who am I? and Who are we? This is to pose then, not merely a dilemma of self-identity; but of self-in-group-identity. . . . Perhaps the answer to developing a total Mexican-American concept must be left in the hands of the artist, the painter, the writer, and the poet, who can abstract the essence of what it is to be Mexican in America. . . . When that understanding comes . . . the Mexican-American will not only have acculturized himself, but he will have acculturized America to him.

14   If anyone knew what he was talking about when he spoke of the dilemma of who he was and where he belonged, it was this Chicano. I very nearly dropped out, as so many other Mexican-Americans have, under the dragging pressure to be someone else, what most of society wants you to be before it hands out its chrome-plated trophies.

15   And that mystique—I didn't quite have it at the time, or the right word for it. But no one did until just the last few years when so many of us stopped trying to be someone else and decided that what we want to be and to be called is Chicano.

16   I owe my life to my Chicano people. They rescued me from the Anglo kiss of death, the monolingual, monocultural, and colorless Gringo society. I no longer face a dilemma of identity or direction. That identity and direction have been charted for me by the Chicano—but to think I came that close to being sucked into the vacuum of the dominant society.

Understanding Meaning

1. What kind of childhood did Rendón have?
2. What represented his early success? What does Rendón mean by the statement "I had bought the white man's world"? What were his goals?
3. What is the "Anglo kiss of death"?
4. How did Rendón respond to people who mispronounced his name?
5. What led to Rendón's transformation?
6. The Chicanos Rendón encountered were the poor of the barrios and bracero camps. Would his sense of identity be different if the Mexicans he encountered in California were affluent Mexican professionals and entrepreneurs?
7. CRITICAL THINKING. Rendón describes the Gringo society as "monolingual, monocultural, and colorless." Does he overlook the diversity of cultures in mainstream America, which includes Jews, the Irish, Italians, Germans, Greeks, Russians, and the French? Is this a perception that people have of any culture, such as that all Mexicans or Nigerians seem alike?

Evaluating Strategy

1. What tone is established in the first sentence? What does the use of the word *victim* indicate?
2. Rendón includes a quote from one of his articles. Is this an effective device?
3. *BLENDING THE MODES.* How does Rendón use narration, description, and comparison in developing "Kiss of Death"?

Appreciating Language

1. What does the term "kiss of death" mean to you? Do you associate it with the Bible or with Hollywood images of the Mafia?
2. Rendón uses several Spanish words without providing definitions in English. What does this suggest about his idea of the United States becoming "acculturized" to Mexican-American culture?
3. Rendón uses both "Mexican-American" and "Chicano." What definitions of these terms are you familiar with? Do "Latino" and "Hispanic" have different meanings and connotations?
4. What does Rendón mean by "cautious Chicanos"?

Writing Suggestions

1. Write your own version of a "kiss of death" you have escaped in your own life. Perhaps you nearly lost yourself or compromised your future by taking a job or entering a relationship you found initially appealing but now view as an error. Your essay should emphasize how you altered your sense of identity.
2. Write a short essay analyzing your role in society. Do you see yourself as an individual in a collective society or as part of a group within society? Do others view you as a member of an ethnic group, one of the disabled, or a product of your neighborhood or generation? Does an in-group identity provide support or heighten your sense of alienation from the greater society?
3. *COLLABORATIVE WRITING.* Discuss Rendón's essay with a group of students, and ask each one to briefly respond to the notion of an "Anglo Kiss of Death." How do members of the group define this? Do they feel it is appropriate or unnecessarily harsh? What does it imply about mainstream American society? Work together to write a few paragraphs expressing the views your group raises. You may organize your statement by using comparison, division, or classification.

RICHARD RODRIGUEZ

Richard Rodriguez (1944–) was born in California of parents who had immigrated from Mexico. Because his parents did not accept that certain neighborhoods in Sacramento were the only options for Mexican Americans, the Rodriguez family lived in a neighborhood that was predominantly Anglo, and he and his siblings attended Catholic school with children from wealthy white families. His first book, the autobiographical Hunger of Memory: The Education of Richard Rodriguez *(1982), deals with his resulting feelings about affirmative action and bilingual education. He went on to write* Mexico's Children *(1991), about Mexicans in America;* Days of Obligation: An Argument with My Mexican Father *(1992); and, most recently,* Brown *(2002). He previously taught, but now is an editor at Pacific News Services, lectures frequently on college campuses and elsewhere, and can be heard on PBS's* Newshour *with Jim Lehrer.*

Aria: A Memoir of a Bilingual Childhood

CONTEXT: *This essay originally appeared in the* American Scholar *and then formed the basis for the first chapter in* Hunger of Memory. *It explains the Rodriguez family's decision to give up speaking Spanish at home in order to give the children a better chance to be successful in English-speaking American schools—and the effects of that decision.*

1   I remember to start with that day in Sacramento—a California now nearly thirty years past—when I first entered a classroom, able to understand some fifty stray English words.

2   The third of four children, I had been preceded to a neighborhood Roman Catholic school by an older brother and sister. But neither of them had revealed very much about their classroom experiences. They left each morning and returned each afternoon, always together, speaking Spanish as they climbed the five steps to the porch. And their mysterious books, wrapped in brown shopping-bag paper, remained on the table next to the door, closed firmly behind them.

3   An accident of geography sent me to a school where all my classmates were white and many were the children of doctors and lawyers and business executives. On that first day of school, my classmates must certainly have been uneasy to find themselves apart from their families, in the first institution of their lives. But I was astonished. I was fated to be the "problem student" in class.

4   The nun said, in a friendly but oddly impersonal voice: "Boys and girls, this is Richard Rodriguez." (I heard her sound *it* out: *Rich-heard Road-ree-guess*.) It was the first time I had heard anyone say my name in English. "Richard," the nun repeated more slowly, writing my name down in her book. Quickly I turned to see my mother's face dissolve in a watery blur behind the pebbled-glass door.

5   Now, many years later, I hear of something called "bilingual education"—a scheme proposed in the late 1960s by Hispanic-American social activists, later endorsed by a congressional vote. It is a program that seeks to permit non-English-speaking children (many from lower class homes) to use their "family language" as the language of school. Such, at least, is the aim its supporters announce. I hear them, and am forced to say no: It is not possible for a child, any child, ever to use his family's language in school. Not to understand this is to misunderstand the public uses of schooling and to trivialize the nature of intimate life.

6   Memory teaches me what I know of these matters. The boy reminds the adult. I was a bilingual child, but of a certain kind: "socially disadvantaged," the son of working-class parents, both Mexican immigrants.

7   In the early years of my boyhood, my parents coped very well in America. My father had steady work. My mother managed at home. They were nobody's victims. When we moved to a house many blocks from the Mexican-American section of town, they were not intimidated by those two or three neighbors who initially tried to make us unwelcome. ("Keep your brats away from my sidewalk!") But despite all they achieved, or perhaps because they had so much to achieve, they lacked any deep feeling of ease, of belonging in public. They regarded the people at work or in crowds as being very distant from us. Those were the others, *los gringos*. That term was interchangeable in their speech with another, even more telling, *los americanos*.

8   I grew up in a house where the only regular guests were my relations. On a certain day, enormous families of relatives would visit us, and there would be so many people that the noise and the bodies would spill out to the backyard and onto the front porch. Then for weeks no one would come. (If the doorbell rang, it was usually a salesman.) Our house stood apart—gaudy yellow in a row of white bungalows. We were the people with the noisy dog, the people who raised chickens. We were the foreigners on the block. A few neighbors would smile and wave at us. We waved back. But until I was seven years old, I did not know the name of the old couple living next door or the names of the kids living across the street.

9   In public, my father and mother spoke a hesitant, accented, and not always grammatical English. And then they would have to strain, their bodies

tense, to catch the sense of what was rapidly said by *los gringos*. At home, they returned to Spanish. The language of their Mexican past sounded in counterpoint to the English spoken in public. The words would come quickly, with ease. Conveyed through those sounds was the pleasing, soothing, consoling reminder that one was at home.

10   During those years when I was first learning to speak, my mother and father addressed me only in Spanish; in Spanish I learned to reply. By contrast, English *(inglés)* was the language I came to associate with *gringos*, rarely heard in the house. I learned my first words of English overhearing my parents speaking to strangers. At six years of age, I knew just enough words for my mother to trust me on errands to stores one block away—but no more.

11   I was then a listening child, careful to hear the very different sounds of Spanish and English. Wide-eyed with hearing, I'd listen to sounds more than to words. First, there were English *(gringo)* sounds. So many words still were unknown to me that when the butcher or the lady at the drugstore said something, exotic polysyllabic sounds would bloom in the midst of their sentences. Often the speech of people in public seemed to me very loud, booming with confidence. The man behind the counter would literally ask, "What can I do for you?" But by being so firm and clear, the sound of his voice said that he was a *gringo;* he belonged in public society. There were also the high, nasal notes of middle-class American speech—which I rarely am conscious of hearing today because I hear them so often, but could not stop hearing when I was a boy. Crowds at Safeway or at bus stops were noisy with the birdlike sounds of *los gringos*. I'd move away from them all—all the chirping chatter above me.

12   My own sounds I was unable to hear, but I knew that I spoke English poorly. My words could not extend to form complete thoughts. And the words I did speak I didn't know well enough to make distinct sounds. (Listeners would usually lower their heads to hear better what I was trying to say.) But it was one thing for *me* to speak English with difficulty; it was more troubling to hear my parents speaking in public: their high-whining vowels and guttural consonants; their sentences that got stuck with "eh" and "ah" sounds; the confused syntax; the hesitant rhythm of sounds so different from the way *gringos* spoke. I'd notice, moreover, that my parents' voices were softer than those of *gringos* we would meet.

13   I am tempted to say now that none of this mattered. (In adulthood I am embarrassed by childhood fears.) And, in a way, it didn't matter very much that my parents could not speak English with ease. Their linguistic difficulties had no serious consequences. My mother and father made themselves understood at the county hospital clinic and at government offices. And yet,

in another way, it mattered very much. It was unsettling to hear my parents struggle with English. Hearing them, I'd grow nervous, and my clutching trust in their protection and power would be weakened.

14   There were many times like the night at a brightly lit gasoline station (a blaring white memory) when I stood uneasily hearing my father talk to a teenage attendant. I do not recall what they were saying, but I cannot forget the sounds my father made as he spoke. At one point his words slid together to form one long word—sounds as confused as the threads of blue and green oil in the puddle next to my shoes. His voice rushed through what he had left to say. Toward the end, he reached falsetto notes, appealing to his listener's understanding. I looked away at the lights of passing automobiles. I tried not to hear anymore. But I heard only too well the attendant's reply, his calm, easy tones. Shortly afterward, headed for home, I shivered when my father put his hand on my shoulder. The very first chance that I got, I evaded his grasp and ran on ahead into the dark, skipping with feigned boyish exuberance.

15   But then there was Spanish: *español*, the language rarely heard away from the house; *español*, the language which seemed to me therefore a private language, my family's language. To hear its sounds was to feel myself specially recognized as one of the family, apart from *los otros*. A simple remark, an inconsequential comment could convey that assurance. My parents would say something to me and I would feel embraced by the sounds of their words. Those sounds said: *I am speaking with ease in Spanish. I am addressing you in words I never use with* los gringos. *I recognize you as someone special, close, like no one outside. You belong with us. In the family. Ricardo.*

16   At the age of six, well past the time when most middle-class children no longer notice the difference between sounds uttered at home and words spoken in public, I had a different experience. I lived in a world compounded of sounds. I was a child longer than most. I lived in a magical world, surrounded by sounds both pleasing and fearful. I shared with my family a language enchantingly private—different from that used in the city around us.

17   Just opening or closing the screen door behind me was an important experience. I'd rarely leave home all alone or without feeling reluctance. Walking down the sidewalk, under the canopy of tall trees, I'd warily notice the (suddenly) silent neighborhood kids who stood warily watching me. Nervously, I'd arrive at the grocery store to hear there the sounds of the *gringos*, reminding me that in this so-big world I was a foreigner. But if leaving home was never routine, neither was coming back. Walking toward our house, climbing the steps from the sidewalk, in summer when the front door was open, I'd hear voices beyond the screen door talking in Spanish. For a second or two I'd stay, linger there listening. Smiling, I'd hear my mother call out,

saying in Spanish, "Is that you, Richard?" Those were her words, but all the while her sounds would assure me: *You are home now. Come close inside. With us.* "*Sí,*" I'd reply.

18 Once more inside the house, I would resume my place in the family. The sounds would grow harder to hear. Once more at home, I would grow less conscious of them. It required, however, no more than the blurt of the doorbell to alert me all over again to listen to sounds. The house would turn instantly quiet while my mother went to the door. I'd hear her hard English sounds. I'd wait to hear her voice turn to soft-sounding Spanish, which assured me, as surely as did the clicking tongue of the lock on the door, that the stranger was gone.

19 Plainly, it is not healthy to hear such sounds so often. It is not healthy to distinguish public from private sounds so easily. I remained cloistered by sounds, timid and shy in public, too dependent on the voices at home. I remember many nights when my father would come back from work, and I'd hear him call out to my mother in Spanish, sounding relieved. In Spanish, his voice would sound the light and free notes that he never could manage in English. Some nights I'd jump up just hearing his voice. My brother and I would come running into the room where he was with our mother. Our laughing (so deep was the pleasure!) became screaming. Like others who feel the pain of public alienation, we transformed the knowledge of our public separateness into a consoling reminder of our intimacy. Excited, our voices joined in a celebration of sounds. *We are speaking now the way we never speak out in public—we are together,* the sounds told me. Some nights no one seemed willing to loosen the hold that sounds had on us. At dinner we invented new words that sounded Spanish, but made sense only to us. We pieced together new words by taking, say, an English verb and giving it Spanish endings. My mother's instructions at bedtime would be lacquered with mock-urgent tones. Or a word like *sí*, sounded in several notes, would convey added measures of feeling. Tongues lingered around the edges of words, especially fat vowels, and we happily sounded that military drum roll, the twirling roar of the Spanish *r*. Family language, my family's sounds: the voices of my parents and sisters and brother. Their voices insisting: *You belong here. We are family members. Related. Special to one another. Listen!* Voices singing and sighing, rising and straining, then surging, teeming with pleasure which burst syllables into fragments of laughter. At times it seemed there was steady quiet only when, from another room, the rustling whispers of my parents faded and I edged closer to sleep.

20 Supporters of bilingual education imply today that students like me miss a great deal by not being taught in their family's language. What they

seem not to recognize is that, as a socially disadvantaged child, I regarded Spanish as a private language. It was a ghetto language that deepened and strengthened my feeling of separateness. What I needed to learn in school was that I had the right, and the obligation, to speak the public language. The odd truth is that my first-grade classmates could have become bilingual, in the conventional sense of the word, more easily than I. Had they been taught early (as upper-middle-class children often are taught) a "second language" like Spanish or French, they could have regarded it simply as another public language. In my case, such bilingualism could not have been so quickly achieved. What I did not believe was that I could speak a single public language.

21   Without question, it would have pleased me to have heard my teachers address me in Spanish when I entered the classroom. I would have felt much less afraid. I would have imagined that my instructors were somehow "related" to me; I would indeed have heard their Spanish as my family's language. I would have trusted them and responded with ease. But I would have delayed—postponed for how long?—having to learn the language of public society. I would have evaded—and for how long?—learning the great lesson of school: that I had a public identity.

22   Fortunately, my teachers were unsentimental about their responsibility. What they understood was that I needed to speak public English. So their voices would search me out, asking me questions. Each time I heard them I'd look up in surprise to see a nun's face frowning at me. I'd mumble, not really meaning to answer. The nun would persist. "Richard, stand up. Don't look at the floor. Speak up. Speak to the entire class, not just to me!" But I couldn't believe English could be my language to use. (In part, I did not want to believe it.) I continued to mumble. I resisted the teacher's demands. (Did I somehow suspect that once I learned this public language my family life would be changed?) Silent, waiting for the bell to sound, I remained dazed, diffident, afraid.

23   Because I wrongly imagined that English was intrinsically a public Language and Spanish was intrinsically private, I easily noted the difference between classroom language and the language at home. At school, words were directed to a general audience of listeners. ("Boys and girls . . .") Words were meaningfully ordered. And the point was not self-expression alone, but to make oneself understood by many others. The teacher quizzed: "Boys and girls, why do we use that word in this sentence? Could we think of a better word to use there? Would the sentence change its meaning if the words were differently arranged? Isn't there a better way of saying much the same thing?" (I couldn't say. I wouldn't try to say.)

24   Three months passed. Five. A half year. Unsmiling, ever watchful, my teachers noted my silence. They began to connect my behavior with the slow progress my brother and sisters were making. Until, one Saturday morning, three nuns arrived at the house to talk to our parents. Stiffly they sat on the blue living-room sofa. From the doorway of another room, spying on the visitors, I noted the incongruity, the clash of two worlds, the faces and voices of school intruding upon the familiar setting of home. I overheard one voice gently wondering, "Do your children speak only Spanish at home, Mrs. Rodriguez?" While another voice added, "That Richard especially seems so timid and shy."

25   *That Rich-heard!*

26   With great tact, the visitors continued, "Is it possible for you and your husband to encourage your children to practice their English when they are home?" Of course my parents complied. What would they not do for their children's well-being? And how could they question the Church's authority which those women represented? In an instant they agreed to give up the language (the sounds) which had revealed and accentuated our family's closeness. The moment after the visitors left, the change was observed. "*Ahora,* speak to us only *en inglés,*" my father and mother told us.

27   At first, it seemed a kind of game. After dinner each night, the family gathered together to practice "our" English. It was still then *inglés,* a language foreign to us, so we felt drawn to it as strangers. Laughing, we would try to define words we could not pronounce. We played with strange English sounds, often overanglicizing our pronunciations. And we filled the smiling gaps of our sentences with familiar Spanish sounds. But that was cheating, somebody shouted, and everyone laughed.

28   In school, meanwhile, like my brother and sisters, I was required to attend a daily tutoring session. I needed a full year of this special work. I also needed my teachers to keep my attention from straying in class by calling out, "*Rich-heard*"—their English voices slowly loosening the ties to my other name, with its three notes, *Ri-car-do.* Most of all, I needed to hear my mother and father speak to me in a moment of seriousness in "broken"— suddenly heartbreaking—English. This scene was inevitable. One Saturday morning I entered the kitchen where my parents were talking, but I did not realize that they were talking in Spanish until, the moment they saw me, their voices changed and they began speaking English. The *gringo* sounds they uttered startled me. Pushed me away. In that moment of trivial misunderstanding and profound insight, I felt my throat twisted by unsounded grief. I simply turned and left the room. But I had no place to escape to

where I could grieve in Spanish. My brother and sisters were speaking English in another part of the house.

29   Again and again in the days following, as I grew increasingly angry, I was obliged to hear my mother and father encouraging me: "Speak to us *en inglés*." Only then did I determine to learn classroom English. Thus, sometime afterward it happened: One day in school, I raised my hand to volunteer an answer to a question. I spoke out in a loud voice and I did not think it remarkable when the entire class understood. That day I moved very far from being the disadvantaged child I had been only days earlier. Taken hold at last was the belief, the calming assurance, that I belonged in public.

30   Shortly after, I stopped hearing the high, troubling sounds of *los gringos*. A more and more confident speaker of English, I didn't listen to *how* strangers sounded when they talked to me. With so many English-speaking people around me, I no longer heard American accents. Conversations quickened. Listening to persons whose voices sounded eccentrically pitched, I might note their sounds for a few seconds, but then I'd concentrate on what they were saying. Now when I heard someone's tone of voice—angry or questioning or sarcastic or happy or sad—I didn't distinguish it from the words it expressed. Sound and word were thus tightly wedded. At the end of each day I was often bemused, and always relieved, to realize how "soundless," though crowded with words, my day in public had been. An eight-year-old boy, I finally came to accept what had been technically true since my birth: I was an American citizen.

31   But diminished by then was the special feeling of closeness at home. Gone was the desperate, urgent, intense feeling of being at home among those with whom I felt intimate. Our family remained a loving family, but one greatly changed. We were no longer so close, no longer bound tightly together by the knowledge of our separateness from *los gringos*. Neither my older brother nor my sisters rushed home after school anymore. Nor did I. When I arrived home, often there would be neighborhood kids in the house. Or the house would be empty of sounds.

32   Following the dramatic Americanization of their children, even my parents grew more publicly confident—especially my mother. First she learned the names of all the people on the block. Then she decided we needed to have a telephone in our house. My father, for his part, continued to use the word gringo, but it was no longer charged with bitterness or distrust. Stripped of any emotional content, the word simply became a name for those Americans not of Hispanic descent. Hearing him, sometimes, I

wasn't sure if he was pronouncing the Spanish word *gringo*, or saying gringo in English.

33 There was a new silence at home. As we children learned more and more English, we shared fewer and fewer words with our parents. Sentences needed to be spoken slowly when one of us addressed our mother or father. Often the parent wouldn't understand. The child would need to repeat himself. Still the parent misunderstood. The young voice, frustrated, would end up saying, "Never mind"—the subject was closed. Dinners would be noisy with the clinking of knives and forks against dishes. My mother would smile softly between her remarks; my father, at the other end of the table, would chew and chew his food while he stared over the heads of his children.

34 My *mother!* My *father!* After English became my primary language, I no longer knew what words to use in addressing my parents. The old Spanish words (those tender accents of sound) I had earlier used—*mamá* and *papá*—I couldn't use anymore. They would have been all-too-painful reminders of how much had changed in my life. On the other hand, the words I heard neighborhood kids call *their* parents seemed equally unsatisfactory. *Mother* and *father*, "ma," "pa," "dad," "pop" (how I hated the all-American sound of that last word)—all these I felt were unsuitable terms of address for *my* parents. As a result, I never used them at home. Whenever I'd speak to my parents, I would try to get their attention by looking at them. In public conversations, I'd refer to them as my "parents" or my "mother" and "father."

35 My mother and father, for their part, responded differently, as their children spoke to them less. My mother grew restless, seemed troubled and anxious at the scarceness of words exchanged in the house. She would question me about my day when I came home from school. She smiled at my small talk. She pried at the edges of my sentences to get me to say something more. ("What . . . ?") She'd join conversations she overheard, but her intrusions often stopped her children's talking. By contrast, my father seemed to grow reconciled to the new quiet. Though his English somewhat improved, he tended more and more to retire into silence. At dinner he spoke very little. One night his children and even his wife helplessly giggled at his garbled English pronunciation of the Catholic "Grace Before Meals." Thereafter he made his wife recite the prayer at the start of each meal, even on formal occasions when there were guests in the house.

36 Hers became the public voice of the family. On official business it was she, not my father, who would usually talk to strangers on the phone or in

stores. We children grew so accustomed to his silence that, years later, we would routinely refer to his "shyness." (My mother often tried to explain: Both of his parents died when he was eight. He was raised by an uncle who treated him as little more than a menial servant. He was never encouraged to speak. He grew up alone. A man of few words.) But I realized my father was not shy, I realized whenever I'd watch him speaking Spanish with relatives. Using Spanish, he was quickly effusive. Especially when talking with other men, his voice would spark, flicker, flare alive with varied sounds. In Spanish, he expressed ideas and feelings he rarely revealed when speaking English. With firm Spanish sounds, he conveyed a confidence and authority that English would never allow him.

37   The silence at home, however, was not simply the result of fewer words, passing between parents and children. More profound for me was the silence created by my inattention to sounds. At about the time I no longer bothered to listen with care to the sounds of English in public, I grew careless about listening to the sounds made by the family when they spoke. Most of the time I would hear someone speaking at home and didn't distinguish his sounds from the words people uttered in public. I didn't even pay much attention to my parents' accented and ungrammatical speech. At least not at home. Only when I was with them in public would I become alert to their accents. But even then their sounds caused me less and less concern. For I was growing increasingly confident of my own public identity.

38   I would have been happier about my public success had I not recalled sometimes, what it had been like earlier, when my family conveyed its intimacy through a set of conveniently private sounds. Sometimes in public, hearing a stranger, I'd hark back to my lost past. A Mexican farm worker approached me one day downtown. He wanted directions to some place. "*Hijito,* . . .?" he said. And his voice stirred old longings. Another time, I was standing beside my mother in the visiting room of a Carmelite convent, before the dense screen which rendered the nuns shadowy figures. I heard several of them speaking Spanish in their busy, singsong, overlapping voices, assuring my mother that, yes, yes, we were remembered, all our family was remembered, in their prayers. Those voices echoed faraway family sounds. Another day, a dark-faced old woman touched my shoulder lightly to steady herself as she boarded a bus. She murmured something to me I couldn't quite comprehend. Her Spanish voice came near, like the face of a never-before-seen relative in the instant before I was kissed. That voice, like so many of the Spanish voices I'd hear in public, recalled the golden age of my childhood.

39   Bilingual educators say today that children lose a degree of "individuality" by becoming assimilated into public society. (Bilingual schooling is a program popularized in the seventies, that decade when middle-class "ethnics" began to resist the process of assimilation—the "American melting pot.") But the bilingualists oversimplify when they scorn the value and necessity of assimilation. They do not seem to realize that a person is individualized in two ways. So they do not realize that, while one suffers a diminished sense of *private* individuality by being assimilated into public society, such assimilation makes possible the achievement of *public* individuality.

40   Simplistically again, the bilingualists insist that a student should he reminded of his difference from others in mass society, of his "heritage." But they equate mere separateness with individuality. The fact is that only in private—with intimates—is separateness from the crowd a prerequisite for individuality; an intimate "tells" me that I am unique, unlike all others, apart from the crowd. In public, by contrast, full individuality is achieved, paradoxically, by those who are able to consider themselves members of the crowd. Thus it happened for me. Only when I was able to think of myself as an American, no longer an alien in *gringo* society, could I seek the rights and opportunities necessary for full public individuality. The social and political advantages I enjoy as a man began on the day I came to believe that my name is indeed *Rich-heard Road-ree-guess*. It is true that my public society today is often impersonal; in fact, my public society is usually mass society. But despite the anonymity of the crowd, and despite the fact that the individuality I achieve in public is often tenuous—because it depends on my being one in a crowd—I celebrate the day I acquired my new name. Those middle-class ethnics who scorn assimilation seem to me filled with decadent self-pity, obsessed by the burden of public life. Dangerously, they romanticize public separateness and trivialize the dilemma of those who are truly socially disadvantaged.

41   If I rehearse here the changes in my private life after my Americanization, it is finally to emphasize a public gain. The loss implies the gain. The house I returned to each afternoon was quiet. Intimate sounds no longer greeted me at the door. Inside there were other noises. The telephone rang. Neighborhood kids ran past the door of the bedroom where I was reading my schoolbooks—covered with brown shopping-bag paper. Once I learned the public language, it would never again be easy for me to hear intimate family voices. More and more of my day was spent hearing words, not sounds. But that may only be a way of saying that on the day I raised my hand in class and spoke loudly to an entire roomful of faces, my childhood started to end.

Understanding Meaning

1.   There is a critical difference for Rodriguez between private and public language, private and public identity. What is the difference? How does this affect his views on bilingual education?
2.   What does Rodriguez consider "the great lesson of school" (paragraph 6)?
3.   What, specifically, triggers the Rodriguez family's decision to speak English at home? What is the immediate effect of the change? What are the long-term effects?
4.   Why is it a turning point for Rodriguez when he enters his family's kitchen one day and his parents switch from speaking Spanish to speaking English?
5.   At what point later does he feel that he has truly become an American citizen? Why?
6.   *CRITICAL THINKING.* Why do many members of ethnic minorities disagree with Rodriguez about his views on bilingual education? Did the Rodriguez family have to make the decision that they did? Have other families chosen a different route and still succeeded? Explain.

Evaluating Strategy

1.   *BLENDING THE MODES.* Although this excerpt from *Hunger of Memory* is a narrative, in it Rodriguez makes extensive use of comparison and contrast. List some of those uses.
2.   In his narrative, Rodriguez focuses on more than one scene. How many different scenes would you say make up this selection? What are they? Why did Rodriguez choose to build this section of his chapter around those mini-narratives?

Appreciating Language

1.   Rodriguez uses this sentence to describe seeing his mother leave as he began his first day of school: "Quickly I turned to see my mother's face dissolve in a watery blur behind the pebbled glass door" (paragraph 4). He has just heard his name spoken in English for the first time. How is Rodriguez using the door as more than simply a physical feature of a classroom?
2.   In paragraph 5, Rodriguez describes himself as "socially disadvantaged." Why does he put that term in quotation marks? Does he feel that he fits the definition of a child who is socially disadvantaged? Why or why not?
3.   What does Rodriguez mean when he uses the terms "private language" and "public language"? Why does he say that he was more aware than

most children of the difference in the *sound* of the two languages? At what point did his awareness of the sound of language change?

4. Rodriguez tells us that he knew only fifty words of English when he started school. He wrote this passage as he was approaching the age of forty. Would you agree that he had come a long way in his skill with English? How would you characterize his writing style?

Writing Suggestions

1. *PREWRITING.* Do you think that members of your own ethnic group feel the same sort of loss associated with education that Rodriguez does? Even if you did not give up your first language to become educated, are there other things that you have chosen to give up by attending college? Explain.

2. *COLLABORATIVE WRITING.* In a paragraph, explain why you agree or disagree with Rodriguez's belief that bilingual education in not in students' best interests. Then share your ideas with the members of your group and see if you can reach a consensus.

3. Write an essay in which you explain how, in a single moment, you knew that something about your family was changed forever. You may want to narrate the one scene in which you came to that realization, or you may want to use other brief scenes to set the stage for that final moment of realization.

DIANE SMITH

Diane Smith is a reporter for the Fort Worth Star-Telegram. *She has published articles on immigration, education, and Texas politics.*

More Immigrants Filling the Ranks of the U.S. Military

CONTEXT: *It has long been recognized that the volunteer army provides upward mobility for American citizens who are having difficulty making it in civilian life. In recent years, the same has proven true for legal immigrants seeking a fast track to citizenship. According to Diane Smith, in April of 2002, the Department of Defense tallied 31,044 noncitizens among the 1.4 million Americans on active duty in the military. (Although illegal immigrants are barred from serving in the military, they must register for the draft.) With increased immigration and the expansion of America's military commitments, this situation is likely to become more pronounced in the future.*

1   Ena Gomez was watching *Sabado Gigante*, a popular Spanish-language variety show, when the words *Ser todo lo que puedes ser* ("Be all you can be") got her attention.

2   A longtime recruiting pitch for the Army, the message inspired Gomez, who was working in fast-food restaurants and hotels in New Jersey but yearning to get a college degree and improve her lot.

3   "I can do that," she told herself.

4   Five years later, the 27-year-old Gomez, a native of Ecuador, is a staff sergeant in the Army, a naturalized U.S. citizen and a mentor to fellow immigrants considering a future in the armed services.

5   From an office in west Fort Worth, she recruits people for the Army.

6   More and more legal immigrants are serving in the military. Some felt compelled to enlist by feelings of patriotism for their adopted homeland. Others are using the military to help pay for their education or meet career goals.

7   Gomez tells immigrant recruits what she told herself when she enlisted: "It's going to cost me a little bit now, but when I'm done, I'll be better off."

8   Immigrants have a long history in the U.S. military, including service in World War II, the Vietnam War and Operation Desert Storm.

9   If the United States goes to war in Iraq, immigrants will have a part in another chapter of U.S. history.

"More Immigrants Filling the Ranks of the U.S. Military" by Diane Smith, December 20, 2002. Reprinted by permission of Tribune Media Services.

10   Many of those on active duty are trying to become naturalized citizens.

11   "Being naturalized or becoming a citizen of the United States gives you a sense of patriotism," said Battalion Chaplain Insoon Jae Gho, who is stationed at Fort Hood.

12   Gho, a native of South Korea, was naturalized in December. Naturalization helps some military personnel prepare for the possibility of war because it gives them a stronger sense of who they are and whom they are serving, Gho said.

13   There are thousands of these immigrants—either naturalized citizens or non-citizens with permanent-residency status—among the 1.4 million people in the military. In April, the Department of Defense tallied 31,044 non-citizens on active duty in the Army, Navy, Air Force and Marines.

14   "They want to be Americans. They want to serve their country," said Master Sgt. James Bulger, master trainer of the Army's Dallas Recruiting Battalion.

15   Bulger, who has recruited people in different parts of the United States, said the U.S. military attracts people from all over the world.

16   Juan Perez joined up in the late 1950s after serving in Mexico's military.

17   "The same day I crossed the border into Texas with my visa, I enlisted in the Air Force. . . . I saw no future over there because I didn't have an education," said Perez, who eventually gained citizenship and advanced in the Air Force.

18   In fiscal 2002, 2,435 foreign-born military personnel were naturalized, up from 1,146 in fiscal 2001, the Immigration and Naturalization Service said.

19   Those figures don't surprise Antonio Gil Morales, commander of the American GI Forum in Tarrant County. The group was founded in 1948 to combat discrimination against Hispanics who had served in World War II.

20   Morales said there has been a push to recruit more Hispanics into the military since the late 1990s. It makes sense that Spanish-speaking immigrants would also step up to serve, he said.

21   "We want more generals," Morales said. "We want more Hispanic people in charge."

22   Non-citizen immigrants who want better positions in the military move quickly for citizenship.

23   "You want to get that rank," Morales said.

24   The military also offers stability and a career.

25   "You get to eat. You get clothing. Plus, you get training," Morales said.

26   Typically, anyone who has served three years in the military and who meets INS citizenship requirements can seek naturalization. But an executive order signed by President Bush in July is speeding up the naturalization of non-citizens on active duty.

27   Under the order, any non-citizen who has served since Sept. 11 is eligible for naturalization.

28   "They are not trying to say 'Join the military and become a citizen,'" said Sgt. 1st Class Richard Barnum, a naturalization specialist at Fort Hood. "They still have to stand on their own merit. They can't violate the good-moral-character criteria."

29   Any immigrant who enlists must now be a legal permanent resident, a status typically described as having a green card. Undocumented immigrants and people with student visas, temporary visas or temporary work permits can't serve in the military.

30   However, male undocumented immigrants ages 18 to 25, like all men in the United States, must register with the Selective Service System.

31   "If there were ever a draft, then the military decides suitability for service," said Alyce Burton, spokeswoman for the Selective Service System in Washington, D.C. The agency is separate from the Defense Department.

32   "We don't know their residency status when they register," she said.

33   Nothing on the registration form indicates a man's status. Non-citizens, who include a variety of statuses, simply leave the spaces for the Social Security number blank.

34   Failure to register could hurt a person's immigration case in the future.

35   "You could be denied citizenship," Burton said.

36   Legal permanent residents can serve no longer than eight years in the military. So those who want a career in the military see citizenship as a means to get better assignments, some involving security clearances unavailable to non-citizens.

37   "Those are the immediate benefits," Barnum said.

38   Rep. Martin Frost, D-Texas, is working on legislation that would make naturalization easier for military personnel. One way is to waive all the fees, which can top $1,000.

39   He also wants to allow the INS to conduct citizenship interviews and hold oath-of-citizenship ceremonies for those deployed at U.S. embassies, consulates and overseas bases.

40   Now, the INS tries to schedule them during the person's leave or around assignments.

41   At Fort Hood, the nation's largest populated military installation, Barnum works closely with soldiers who want to gain citizenship. Every Tuesday morning, he conducts a seminar to help them maneuver through INS paperwork. In the past 18 months, 1,070 men and women on active duty at the base have been naturalized or have begun the process of gaining citizenship.

42   Applicants must undergo military and INS checks, said Wiley Blakeway of the San Antonio district of the INS. The district handles 200 to 400

naturalization cases a year for the nine military installations in that district, which includes Fort Hood.

43   For Gho, joining the military was a way to give back to the United States and to follow a calling to serve in God's ministry.

44   "It's more like my gratitude to those soldiers who died during the Korean War and their families," she said.

45   Immigrants' desire to serve is not always apparent to those who don't rub shoulders with them, said Gomez, the Army recruiter from Ecuador. After the Sept. 11 terrorist attacks, some immigrants told her that they wanted to defend the United States. Many were ineligible to serve because they were undocumented.

46   "They are people who have no papers," Gomez said.

47   She said some immigrants come to the recruiting office to ask questions or to take a practice version of the pre-enlistment math and English skills test. Failure to pass the test can keep them out of the military, as can criminal histories.

48   Many immigrants must weigh their loyalty to their native lands against their service to the United States, Gomez said. But once they take the oath, they are Americans.

49   "The opportunities we have here we don't have in our countries. I love my (home) country, but you don't bite the hand that feeds you," Gomez said. "This country gave me my house, my car."

50   Lizeth Serrano said she is ready to join the ranks. An immigrant from Mexico, the 17-year-old senior at Diamond Hill-Jarvis High School in Fort Worth became a U.S. citizen in July and recently enlisted in the Army.

51   She said the military offers a chance to get a college education and to pursue a career in photography.

52   "I want to meet different people. I want to get out of here, see other places," said Serrano, her words moving comfortably from Spanish to English.

53   And if there's a war?

54   "I'll go kick some butt," she joked.

Understanding Meaning

1.   According to this article, what are some of the practical reasons that immigrants enlist in the military? Is every immigrant eligible for military service?
2.   What are some of the intangible reasons?
3.   Why are young men who are not citizens required to register for the draft?

4. What plans are there for making it easier for those who are enlisted to seek citizenship?

5. What does Smith mean when she quotes Gomez as saying, "Many immigrants must weigh their loyalty to their native lands against their service to the United States"?

6. *CRITICAL THINKING.* Some countries require military service of all young men—and in some cases of all young women as well. Do you feel that the United States should adopt such a requirement? Why or why not?

Evaluating Strategy

1. *BLENDING THE MODES.* What rationale does Smith seem to have had for choosing the particular examples that she did? (Consider what each one adds to the points that she is trying to make.)

2. What types of support, other than examples, does the author make use of?

3. What do the direct quotations add to the effectiveness of the essay?

Appreciating Language

1. Does Smith use objective or subjective language in talking about immigrants in the military?

2. What is the tone of the piece, or the writer's attitude towards her subject?

Writing Suggestions

1. Do you feel that it is good to broaden diversity in the military by including larger numbers of immigrants? Why or why not?

2. How is service in the military related to the idea of the American dream that draws so many immigrants to the United States?

3. In the aftermath of the bombing of Pearl Harbor on December 7, 1941, young Americans of Japanese descent were given the option of enlisting in the armed forces of the United States. Why was the decision they had to make such a difficult one?

4. *COLLABORATIVE WRITING.* Exchange the essay you wrote for Writing Suggestion #1, #2, or #3 above with a classmate. Return the essay to the author with a written response explaining how convincing his or her argument is and where it might be strengthened.

GEORGE SOROS

George Soros (1930–) was born in Budapest, Hungary, and emigrated to England in 1947. After receiving a BS degree from the London School of Economics, he moved to New York in 1956. After working as a financial trader and analyst, he founded the Soros Fund Management. Soros is noted for his success in investment management and his extensive philanthropy. He has created a number of foundations in Eastern Europe to help build educational, economic, and cultural institutions. He is the author of The Alchemy of Finance *(1987) and* Ideas and Actions *(1995).*

America's Global Role: Why the Fight for a Worldwide Open Society Begins at Home

CONTEXT: *George Soros has donated millions of dollars to help develop educational and cultural institutions around the world. He has devoted much of his attention to helping reform and democratize the former communist countries of Eastern Europe.*

1 On May 27, 1999, at the invitation of then-Dean Paul Wolfowitz, I delivered a commencement address at the Paul H. Nitze School of Advanced International Studies in Washington. I spoke about my vision for a global open society and Wolfowitz, now deputy secretary of defense, seemed to be on the same wavelength. We had both participated in a small group called The Action Council for the Balkans, which was agitating for a more muscular policy against Slobodan Milosevic. We advocated military intervention in Bosnia much sooner than it happened. I remember a lively exchange with Colin Powell when I questioned the Powell doctrine of "we do deserts but we don't do mountains." I was very supportive of Madeleine Albright's activism on Kosovo, where I was in favor of a coalition of the willing: NATO intervention without United Nations authorization.

2 On March 7, 2003, on the eve of war with Iraq, I gave another speech at the same graduate school. This article is adapted from that speech. I was then and continue to be in favor of the removal from power of Saddam Hussein, who was, because of his chemical and biological weapons, an even more dangerous despot than Milosevic. I would like to see regime change in many other places. I am particularly concerned about Zimbabwe, where Robert Mugabe's regime is going from bad to worse. I also see Muammar

Quaddafi as a dangerous troublemaker in Africa. I support a project on Burma, or Myanmar as it is now called, which backs Aung San Suu Kyi as the democratically elected leader. I have foundations in central Asia, and I would like to see regime change in countries such as Turkmenistan. And, of course, I hoped for an easy victory in Iraq, if we went to war at all.

3   Yet I am profoundly opposed to the Bush administration's policies, not only in Iraq but altogether. My opposition is much more profound than it was in the case of the Clinton administration. I believe the Bush administration is leading the United States and the world in the wrong direction. In the past, my philanthropy focused on defeating communism and helping with the transition from closed societies to open societies in the former Soviet empire. Now I would go so far as to say that the fight for a global open society has to be fought in the United States. In short, America ought to play a very different role in the world than it is playing today.

4   Because open society is an abstract idea, I shall proceed from the abstract and general to the concrete and particular. The concept of "open society" was developed by philosopher Karl R. Popper, whose book *Open Society and Its Enemies* argued that totalitarian ideologies—such as communism and fascism—posed a threat to an open society because they claimed to have found the final solution. The ultimate truth is beyond human reach. Those who say they are in possession of it are making a false claim, and they can enforce it only by coercion and repression. So Popper derived the principles of freedom and democracy—the same principles that President Bush championed in his February speech on Iraq—from the recognition that we may be wrong.

5   That brings us to the crux of the matter. Bush makes absolutely no allowance for the possibility that we may be wrong, and he has no tolerance for dissenting opinion. If you are not with us you are against us, he proclaims. Donald Rumsfeld berates our European allies who disagree with him on Iraq in no uncertain terms, and he has a visceral aversion to international cooperation, be it with NATO or UN peacekeepers in Afghanistan. And John Ashcroft accuses those who opposed the USA Patriot Act of giving aid and comfort to the enemy. These are the views of extremists, not adherents to an open society. Perhaps because of my background, these views push the wrong buttons in me. And I am amazed and disappointed that the general public does not have a similar allergic reaction. Of course, that has a lot to do with September 11.

6   But the trouble goes much deeper. It is not merely that the Bush administration's policies may be wrong, it is that they are wrong, and I would go even further: They are bound to be wrong because they are based on a

false ideology. A dominant faction within the Bush administration believes that international relations are relations of power. Because we are unquestionably the most powerful, they claim, we have earned the right to impose our will on the rest of the world.

7   This position is enshrined in the Bush doctrine that was first enunciated in the president's speech at West Point in June 2002 and then incorporated in the National Security Strategy last September.

8   The Bush doctrine is built on two pillars: First, the United States will do everything in its power to maintain its unquestioned military supremacy, and second, the United States arrogates the right to preemptive action. Taken together, these two pillars support two classes of sovereignty: the sovereignty of the United States, which takes precedence over international treaties and obligations, and the sovereignty of all other states, which is subject to the Bush doctrine. This is reminiscent of George Orwell's *Animal Farm:* All animals are equal but some are more equal than others.

9   To be sure, the Bush doctrine is not stated so starkly; it is buried in Orwellian doublespeak. The doublespeak is needed because there is a contradiction between the Bush administration's concepts of freedom and democracy and the principles of open society.

10   In an open society, people can decide for themselves what they mean by freedom and democracy. But the Bush administration claims that we have discovered the ultimate truth. The very first sentence of our latest National Security Strategy reads as follows:

11   "The great struggles of the twentieth century between liberty and totalitarianism ended with a decisive victory for the forces of freedom—and a single sustainable model for national success: freedom, democracy, and free enterprise."

12   This statement is false on two counts. First, there is no single, sustainable model for national success. And second, our model, which has been successful, is not available to others because our success depends greatly on our dominant position at the center of the global capitalist system, and that position is not attainable by others.

13   According to the ideologues of the far right, who currently dominate the Bush administration, the success of the American model has been brought about by a combination of market fundamentalism in economic matters and the pursuit of military supremacy in international relations. These two objectives fit neatly together into a coherent ideology—an ideology that is internally consistent but does not jibe with reality or with the principles of open society. It is a kind of crude social Darwinism in which the survival of the fittest depends on competition, not cooperation. In the economy, the

competition is among firms; in international relations, among states. Cooperation does not seem necessary because there is supposed to be an invisible hand at work that will ensure that as long as everybody looks out for his or her own interests, the common interest will look after itself.

14   This doctrine is false, even with regard to the economy. Financial markets left to their own devices do not tend toward an equilibrium that guarantees the optimum allocation of resources. The theories of efficient markets and rational expectations don't stand up to critical examination. But at least these theories exist, and they are widely accepted.

15   No similar theory can reasonably be proposed with regard to international relations. There is the well-known doctrine of geopolitical realism according to which states have interests but no principles. But nobody can deny that there are common human interests that transcend national interests.

16   We live in an increasingly interdependent world and, due to the progress of technology, our power over nature has increased by leaps and bounds. Unless we use that power wisely, we are in danger of damaging or destroying both our environment and our civilization. These are not empty words. Terrorism and the spread of weapons of mass destruction give us a taste of what lies ahead. The need for a better world order predates September 11, but the terrorist threat has rendered international cooperation all the more necessary.

17   That is not how the Bush administration sees the world. Its perspective is not totally false but it emphasizes one aspect of reality to the exclusion of others. The aspect it stresses is power, and in particular military power. But military power is not the only kind of power; no empire could ever be held together by military power alone. Joseph S. Nye Jr., in his recent book *The Paradox of American Power*, introduced the concept of "soft power" to bring the point home.

18   I would go even further. Applying the concept of power to human affairs is altogether questionable. In physics, power or force governs the behavior of objects. That is a misleading analogy for human affairs. People have a will of their own. They may be cowed by military power or other forms of repression, but that is not a sound principle of social organization. Might is not right.

19   Yet that is the belief that guides the Bush administration. Israel's Ariel Sharon shares the same belief, and look where that has led. The idea that might is right cannot be reconciled with the idea of an open society.

20   The objective of disarming Saddam Hussein was a valid one, but the way the U.S. government has gone about it is not. That is why there was so much

opposition to the war throughout the world and at home. That is why I shall remain opposed to the Bush administration's conduct of foreign policy.

21   There is an alternative vision of the role that the United States ought to play in the world, and it is based on the concept of open society. The current world order is a distorted form of a global open society. It is distorted because we have global markets but we do not have global political institutions. As a consequence, we are much better at producing private goods than taking care of public goods such as preserving peace, protecting the environment and ensuring economic stability, progress and social justice. This is not by accident.

22   Globalization—and by that I mean the globalization of financial markets—was a market fundamentalist project, and the United States was its chief architect. We are also the chief beneficiary. We are unquestionably the dominant power in the world today. Our dominance is not only economic and financial but also military and technological. No other country can even come close to us.

23   This puts us in a position of unique responsibility. Other countries have to respond to U.S. policy, but the United States is in a position to choose the policy to which others have to respond. We have a greater degree of discretion than anybody else in deciding what shape the world should take. Therefore it is not enough for the United States to preserve its supremacy over other states; it must also concern itself with the well-being of the world.

24   There were great tensions in the global capitalist system prior to September 11, but they have gotten much worse since then. We must work to reduce the tensions and make the system stable and equitable so that we can maintain our dominant position within it.

25   That is the responsibility that we fail to live up to. Worse, the Bush administration does not even acknowledge that we bear such a responsibility. It attributes our dominant position to the success of the American model in fair competition with other countries. But that is a self-deception.

26   Contrary to the tenets of market fundamentalism, the global capitalist system does not constitute a level playing field. In economic and financial matters, there is a disparity between the center and the periphery. And in military matters, there is a disparity between the United States and the rest of the world because the European Union, as distinct from its member states, does not seek to be a military power. There are large and growing inequalities in the world, and we lack the mechanism for reducing them. Therefore we need to strengthen our international political institutions to match the globalization of our markets. Only the United States can lead the

way because without U.S. participation, nothing much can be done in the way of international cooperation.

27   A world order based on the sovereignty of states, moreover, cannot take care of our common human interests. The main source of poverty and misery in the world today is bad government—repressive, corrupt regimes and failed states. And yet it is difficult to intervene in the internal affairs of other countries because the principle of sovereignty stands in the way.

28   One way to overcome the problem is to offer countries positive inducements for becoming open societies. That is the missing ingredient in the current world order. There are penalties for bad behavior, from trade sanctions to military intervention, but not enough incentives and reinforcements for good behavior. A global open society would achieve certain standards by providing assistance to those who are unable to meet them. States that violate the standards could be punished through exclusion. There would be a better balance between rewards and reinforcements on the one hand and penalties on the other. In a global open society, every country would benefit from belonging to it. Developing countries would get better access to markets under the World Trade Organization. Countries at the periphery, such as Brazil, would be guaranteed an adequate supply of credit through the International Monetary Fund as long as they followed sound policies, and there would be a genuine attempt to meet the UN's millennium goals of reducing poverty and improving lives throughout the world.

29   Providing incentives, of course, would not be sufficient. Not all countries have governments that want or tolerate an open society. A rogue regime such as Saddam Hussein's was a threat to the rest of the world, and a global open society must be able to defend itself. But the use of military force must remain a last resort.

30   The United States cannot create a global open society on its own. No single country can act as the police officer or the benefactor of the entire world. But a global open society cannot be achieved without American leadership. This means that the United States must engage in international cooperation. It must be willing to abide by the rules it seeks to impose on others, to accept its share of the costs and, most importantly, to accept that other participants are bound to have other opinions, and other states other national interests. The United States will always have veto rights due to its weight and importance.

31   Here is an alternative vision of America's role in the world. It is the vision of America leading the world toward a global open society. Such a vision is badly needed. After September 11, President Bush has managed to convince the country that it is unpatriotic to disagree with him.

32   The two visions—American supremacy and America as the leader of a global open society—are not that far apart. In fact, they are so close to each other that I am afraid that when the pursuit of American supremacy fails—as it is bound to fail—the vision of a global open society will also be abandoned. That is why it is so important to distinguish between them.

33   Both visions recognize the dominant position of the United States. Both agree that the United States has to take an active leadership role in international affairs. Both favor preemptive action. But when it comes to the kind of preemptive action that America ought to take, the two visions differ. A global open society requires affirmative action on a global scale while the Bush approach is restricted to punitive action. In the open-society version, crisis prevention cannot start early enough; it is impossible to predict which grievance will develop into bloodshed, and by the time we know, it is too late. That is why the best way to prevent conflicts is to foster open societies.

34   The Bush administration claims to be fostering democracy by invading Iraq. But democracy cannot be imposed from the outside. I have been actively involved in building open societies in a number of countries through my network of foundations. Speaking from experience, I would never choose Iraq for nation building.

35   Military occupation is the easy part; what comes afterward is what should give us pause. The internal tensions and the external ones with neighboring countries such as Turkey and Iran will make it very difficult to establish a democratic Iraqi regime. To impose a military regime as Douglas MacArthur did in post–World War II Japan would be to court disaster.

36   It would have been easier to achieve success in Afghanistan because both the Taliban and al-Qaeda were alien oppressors. But having won a resounding military victory, we failed to follow through with nation building. Secretary Rumsfeld opposed the extension of UN peacekeeping beyond Kabul, and, as a result, law and order have still not been fully established outside the capital. Hamid Karzai needs to be protected by American bodyguards. His government is making slow progress, but the historic opportunity to build on the momentum of liberation was irretrievably lost.

37   The war with Iraq does not help the building of open societies in other countries, either. In our efforts to gain allies and buy votes in the United Nations, we have become less concerned with internal conditions in those countries than we ought to be. This is true of Russia and Pakistan and all the central Asian republics, not to mention Angola and Cameroon, which are among the most corrupt regimes in Africa. To claim that we are invading Iraq for the sake of establishing democracy is a sham, and the rest of the

world sees it as such. The Atlantic Alliance has been severely disrupted, and both NATO and the European Union are in disarray.

38   Disarming Iraq is a valid objective, but with regard to weapons of mass destruction, Iraq ought not to be the top priority today. North Korea is much more dangerous, and it has to be said that President Bush precipitated the current crisis. North Korea's nuclear program had been more or less contained in 1994 by the Agreed Framework concluded by the Clinton administration. In the meantime, President Kim Dae Jung of South Korea had engaged in a sunshine policy, and it began to bear fruit. There was progress in removing land mines along the border, and a direct train connection was about to be opened. The North Korean leadership seemed to become increasingly aware that it needed economic reforms.

39   When Kim Dae Jung came to Washington as the first foreign head of state to visit President Bush, he wanted to enlist the president's support for the sunshine policy. But Bush rebuffed him rather brusquely and publicly. Bush disapproved of what he regarded as the appeasement of North Korea, and he was eager to establish a discontinuity with the Clinton administration. He also needed North Korea out in the cold in order to justify the first phase of the National Missile Defense program, the initial linchpin in the Bush strategy of asserting U.S. supremacy. Then came the "axis of evil" speech, and when North Korea surprised the Bush administration by admitting its uranium-enrichment program (strictly speaking not in violation of the Agreed Framework because that covered only plutonium), Bush cut off the supply of fuel oil. North Korea responded with various provocations.

40   As this magazine goes to press, North Korea could soon start producing a nuclear bomb a month. In mid-April, it backed off its demand for bilateral talks with the United States and agreed to three-way talks with the United States and China. But a serious rift between the United States and South Korea remains. South Koreans now regard the United States as being as much of an aggressor as North Korea, and this renders our position very difficult.

41   The Bush administration's policies have brought about many unintended, adverse consequences. Indeed, it is difficult to find a similar time span during which political and economic conditions have deteriorated as rapidly as they have in the last couple of years.

42   But the game is not yet over. The quick victory in Iraq could bring about a dramatic change in the overall situation. The price of oil could fall, the stock market could celebrate, consumers could overcome their anxieties and resume spending, and business could respond by stepping up capital expenditures. The United States could reduce its dependency on Saudi Arabia, the Israeli-Palestinian conflict could become more tractable

and negotiations with North Korea could calm tensions with Pyongyang. That is what the Bush administration is counting on.

43 The jury is out. But whatever the outcome in Iraq, I predict that the Bush approach is bound to fail eventually because it is based on false premises. I base my prediction on my theory of reflexivity and my study of boom-bust processes, or bubbles, in the financial markets.

44 Bubbles do not grow out of thin air. They have a solid basis in reality, but misconception distorts reality. In this case, the dominant position of the United States is the reality, the pursuit of American supremacy the misconception. For a while, reality can reinforce the misconception, but eventually it is bound to become unsustainable. During the self-reinforcing phase, the misconception seems irresistible but, unless it is corrected earlier, a dramatic reversal becomes inevitable. The later it comes the more devastating the consequences. There seems to be an inexorable quality about the course of events, but, of course, a boom-bust process can be aborted at any stage. Most stock-market booms are aborted long before the extremes of the recent bull market are reached. The sooner it happens, the better. That is how I feel about the Bush doctrine.

45 I firmly believe that President Bush is leading the United States and the world in the wrong direction and I consider it nothing short of tragic that the terrorist threat has induced the country to line up behind him so uncritically. The Bush administration came into office with an unsound and eventually unsustainable ideology. Prior to September 11, it could not make much headway in implementing its ideology because it lacked a clear mandate and a clearly defined enemy. September 11 changed all that. The terrorist attack removed both constraints.

46 Terrorism is the ideal enemy because it is invisible and therefore never disappears. Having an enemy that poses a genuine and widely recognized threat can be very effective in holding the nation together. That is particularly useful when the prevailing ideology is based on the unabashed pursuit of self-interest. By declaring war on terrorism, President Bush gained the mandate he had previously lacked to pursue his goals. The Bush administration is deliberately fostering fear because it helps to keep the nation lined up behind the president. We have come a long way from Franklin Delano Roosevelt, who said that we have nothing to fear but fear itself.

47 But the war on terrorism—which is supposed to include the war on Iraq—cannot be accepted as the guiding principle of our foreign policy. What will happen to the world if the most powerful country on earth—the one that sets the agenda—is solely preoccupied with self-preservation?

America must play a more constructive role if humanity is to make any progress.

48   Acting as the leader of a global open society will not protect the United States from terrorist attacks. But by playing a constructive role, we can regain the respect and support of the world, and this will make the task of fighting terrorism easier.

49   The Bush vision of American supremacy is not only unsound and unsustainable, it is also in contradiction with American values. We are an open society. The principles of open society are enshrined in the Declaration of Independence. And the institutions of our democracy are protected by our Constitution. The fact that we have a bunch of far-right ideologues in our executive branch does not turn us into a totalitarian dictatorship. There are checks and balances, and the president must obtain the support of the people. I put my faith in the people. But in the end, open society will not survive unless those who live in it believe in it.

Understanding Meaning

1.   How does Soros define an "open society"? How does an open society differ from a totalitarian society?
2.   Why does Soros argue that the Bush administration's ideology is wrong?
3.   What two pillars is the Bush doctrine based on in Soros's view? Why does he believe the doctrine is wrong?
4.   According to Soros, what responsibility does the United States have in the 21st century? What does he see as its proper role in international affairs?
5.   Why does Soros see American participation in the world as necessary to create international cooperation?
6.   How does Soros believe democracy can be fostered around the world? Why does he feel that establishing a democracy in Iraq will be more difficult than establishing a democracy in Afghanistan would have been?
7.   *CRITICAL THINKING.* Why does Soros believe that the guiding principle of American foreign policy cannot be a war on terrorism? Is a war on terrorism a simple preoccupation with self-preservation, or can a war on terrorism also include efforts to alleviate the causes of terrorism, such as poverty, oppression, unemployment, and extremism?

Evaluating Strategy

1.   Do you find Soros's opening effective? Does mentioning previous addresses and previous statements give a writer greater authority or make the argument seem personal and opinionated?

2. Soros disagrees strongly with current American policies, but does his alternative seem realistic?
3. What evidence does Soros present to support his thesis? Is it convincing?
4. *CRITICAL THINKING.* What strategies can a writer use to criticize current policies and advance alternative ideas without alienating those who support the president or believe we must wage a war on terrorism?

Appreciating Language

1. What connotations does the term *open society* have? Do all people see this as desirable? To some, will "open" suggest a dangerous departure from tradition or religious doctrine?
2. Soros blames many of the problems of the world on the principle of sovereignty. What does *sovereignty* mean? Why does Soros see it as a problem in the 21st century?

Writing Suggestions

1. Write a brief essay that supports or criticizes Soros's position on the war on terrorism and creating open societies. What, in your opinion, constitutes success?
2. *COLLABORATIVE WRITING.* Discuss Soros's article with other students. Work together and develop a list of actions individuals can take to help advance an open society at home and abroad.

AMY TAN

Amy Tan (1952–) was born in Oakland, California, the daughter of Chinese immigrants who came to America in the late 1940s. Her first book of fiction, a collection of interrelated stories called The Joy Luck Club, *was an immediate best seller in 1989. It was followed by three novels,* The Kitchen God's Wife *(1991),* The Hundred Secret Senses *(1995), and* The Bonesetter's Daughter *(2001), and a children's book,* The Moon Lady *(1992).*

Fish Cheeks

CONTEXT: *This story is set in 1966, when Amy Tan was fourteen. As the American-born daughter of a Chinese family, Tan is caught between her ties to her parents' culture and her desire to fit into the mainstream of American life. This dilemma is symbolized by her crush on the minister's blond-haired son. Only in the final paragraph of this selection (which originally appeared in* Seventeen *magazine in 1987) do we get Tan's adult perspective on this situation.*

1   I fell in love with the minister's son the winter I turned fourteen. He was not Chinese, but as white as Mary in the manger. For Christmas I prayed for this blond-haired boy, Robert, and a slim new American nose.

2   When I found out that my parents had invited the minister's family over for Christmas Eve dinner, I cried. What would Robert think of our shabby Chinese Christmas? What would he think of our noisy Chinese relatives who lacked proper American manners? What terrible disappointment would he feel upon seeing not a roasted turkey and sweet potatoes but Chinese food?

3   On Christmas Eve I saw that my mother had outdone herself in creating a strange menu. She was pulling black veins out of the backs of fleshy prawns. The kitchen was littered with appalling mounds of raw food: A slimy rock cod with bulging eyes that pleaded not to be thrown into a pan of hot oil. Tofu, which looked like stacked wedges of rubbery white sponges. A bowl soaking dried fungus back to life. A plate of squid, their backs crisscrossed with knife markings so they resembled bicycle tires.

4   And then they arrived—the minister's family and all my relatives in a clamor of doorbells and rumpled Christmas packages. Robert grunted hello, and I pretended he was not worthy of existence.

5   Dinner threw me deeper into despair. My relatives licked the ends of their chopsticks and reached across the table, dipping them into the dozen or so plates of food. Robert and his family waited patiently for platters to be passed to them. My relatives murmured with pleasure when my mother brought out the whole steamed fish. Robert grimaced. Then my father poked his chopsticks just below the fish eye and plucked out the soft meat. "Amy, your favorite," he said, offering me the tender fish cheek. I wanted to disappear.

6   At the end of the meal my father leaned back and belched loudly, thanking my mother for her fine cooking. "It's a polite Chinese custom to show you are satisfied," explained my father to our astonished guests. Robert was looking down at his plate with a reddened face. The minister managed to muster up a quiet burp. I was stunned into silence for the rest of the night.

7   After everyone had gone, my mother said to me, "You want to be the same as American girls on the outside." She handed me an early gift. It was a miniskirt in beige tweed. "But inside you must always be Chinese. You must be proud you are different. Your only shame is to have shame."

8   And even though I didn't agree with her then, I knew that she understood how much I had suffered during the evening's dinner. It wasn't until many years later—long after I had gotten over my crush on Robert—that I was able to fully appreciate her lesson and the true purpose behind our particular menu. For Christmas Eve that year, she had chosen all my favorite foods.

Understanding Meaning

1.   Amy Tan has written often about how it feels to be caught between two cultures. Explain how this short narrative illustrates the tension between two cultures that she felt as a teenager.

2.   What was it about the dinner that made Tan feel such embarrassment?

3.   Immediately after the dinner, Tan's mother wisely pointed out the need for her daughter to accept both cultures of which she was a part. How did she show that she understood the clash between the two worlds that her daughter experienced?

4.   Only years later did Tan understand the menu served that night. Why did Tan's mother prepare those particular foods?

5.   CRITICAL THINKING. Entering college often brings a student in contact with unfamiliar cultures, even if they are not as different from his or her home culture as for Tan. Explain how the differences between cultures can lead to awkwardness and embarrassment.

Evaluating Strategy

1. In this brief narrative, Tan chose to put the thesis at the end. Why was that an appropriate choice for this piece?
2. "Fish Cheeks" was originally published in *Seventeen*, a magazine read primarily by teenage girls. As an adult looking back on her teenage years, Tan was still able to include details girls could relate to. What are some of those details?
3. *BLENDING THE MODES.* Which paragraphs provide good models of a topic sentence supported by specific examples?
4. What was Tan's rationale for dividing her essay into paragraphs as she did? Why are the paragraph breaks appropriately placed?

Appreciating Language

1. In her first paragraph, Tan writes, "For Christmas I prayed for this blond-haired boy, Robert, and a slim new American nose." What is the effect of linking the two in the same prayer?
2. What specific words in the essay appeal to the various senses?
3. How do you interpret this statement by Tan's mother: "You must be proud you are different. Your only shame is to have shame" (paragraph 7)?

Writing Suggestions

1. Using Tan's essay as a model, write a narrative based on your own experience in which you tell about an event and at the end make clear what the event's significance was.
2. Sometimes, like Tan, we do not fully realize the significance of an event until much later. Choose such an event from your past and narrate the event, making clear by the end what you finally realized about its significance.
3. *COLLABORATIVE WRITING.* Brainstorm with your group about ways in which entering college brings you in contact with different cultures and traditions. Think not only about meeting people from different countries or ethnic groups but also about how people from different parts of the country or of different religious faiths bring diversity to a college campus.
4. Rewrite "Fish Cheeks" from the point of view of Robert.

DEBORAH TANNEN

A native of Brooklyn, New York, Deborah Tannen (1945–) is a professor of linguistics at Georgetown University. She has written widely on the effect of gender on communication in such popular periodicals as the New York Times Magazine, New York *magazine, and the* Washington Post. *Her many books include* That's Not What I Meant *(1986) and* You Just Don't Understand: Women and Men in Conversation *(1990).*

Sex, Lies and Conversation: Why Is It So Hard for Men and Women to Talk to Each Other?

CONTEXT: *With increased participation in the business world, women have had to deal with the issue of communication in the workplace on new levels and in new contexts. The subject of whether there are gender differences in workplace communication has interested a range of experts, including Tannen. Here, however, she looks specifically at how men and women take on different roles in communication at home than they do in public.*

1   I was addressing a small gathering in a suburban Virginia living room—a women's group that had invited men to join them. Throughout the evening, one man had been particularly talkative, frequently offering ideas and anecdotes, while his wife sat silently beside him on the couch. Toward the end of the evening, I commented that women frequently complain that their husbands don't talk to them. This man quickly concurred. He gestured toward his wife and said, "She's the talker in our family." The room burst into laughter; the man looked puzzled and hurt. "It's true," he explained. "When I come home from work I have nothing to say. If she didn't keep the conversation going, we'd spend the whole evening in silence."

2   This episode crystallizes the irony that although American men tend to talk more than women in public situations, they often talk less at home. And this pattern is wreaking havoc with marriage.

3   The pattern was observed by political scientist Andrew Hacker in the late '70s. Sociologist Catherine Kohler Riessman reports in her new book *Divorce Talk* that most of the women she interviewed—but only a few of the men—gave lack of communication as the reason for their divorces. Given the current divorce rate of nearly 50 percent, that amounts to millions of cases in the United States every year—a virtual epidemic of failed conversation.

4   In my own research, complaints from women about their husbands most often focused not on tangible inequities such as having given up the

chance for a career to accompany a husband to his, or doing far more than their share of daily life-support work like cleaning, cooking, social arrangements and errands. Instead, they focused on communication: "He doesn't listen to me," "He doesn't talk to me." I found, as Hacker observed years before, that most wives want their husbands to be, first and foremost, conversational partners, but few husbands share this expectation of their wives.

5   In short, the image that best represents the current crisis is the stereotypical cartoon scene of a man sitting at the breakfast table with a newspaper held up in front of his face, while a woman glares at the back of it, wanting to talk.

Linguistic Battle of the Sexes

6   How can women and men have such different impressions of communication in marriage? Why the widespread imbalance in their interests and expectations?

7   In the April [1990] issue of *American Psychologist,* Stanford University's Eleanor Maccoby reports the results of her own and others' research showing that children's development is most influenced by the social structure of peer interactions. Boys and girls tend to play with children of their own gender, and their sex-separate groups have different organizational structures and interactive norms.

8   I believe these systematic differences in childhood socialization make talk between women and men like cross-cultural communication, heir to all the attraction and pitfalls of that enticing but difficult enterprise. My research on men's and women's conversations uncovered patterns similar to those described for children's groups.

9   For women, as for girls, intimacy is the fabric of relationships, and talk is the thread from which it is woven. Little girls create and maintain friendships by exchanging secrets; similarly, women regard conversation as the cornerstone of friendship. So a woman expects her husband to be a new and improved version of a best friend. What is important is not the individual subjects that are discussed but the sense of closeness, of a life shared, that emerges when people tell their thoughts, feelings, and impressions.

10   Bonds between boys can be as intense as girls', but they are based less on talking, more on doing things together. Since they don't assume talk is the cement that binds a relationship, men don't know what kind of talk women want, and they don't miss it when it isn't there.

11   Boys' groups are larger, more inclusive, and more hierarchical, so boys must struggle to avoid the subordinate position in the group. This may play

a role in women's complaints that men don't listen to them. Some men really don't like to listen, because being the listener makes them feel one-down, like a child listening to adults or an employee to a boss.

12 But often when women tell men, "You aren't listening," and the men protest, "I am," the men are right. The impression of not listening results from misalignments in the mechanics of conversation. The misalignment begins as soon as a man and a woman take physical positions. This became clear when I studied videotapes made by psychologist Bruce Dorval of children and adults talking to their same-sex best friends. I found that at every age, the girls and women faced each other directly, their eyes anchored on each other's faces. At every age, the boys and men sat at angles to each other and looked elsewhere in the room, periodically glancing at each other. They were obviously attuned to each other, often mirroring each other's movements. But the tendency of men to face away can give women the impression they aren't listening even when they are. A young woman in college was frustrated: Whenever she told her boyfriend she wanted to talk to him, he would lie down on the floor, close his eyes, and put his arm over his face. This signaled to her, "He's taking a nap." But he insisted he was listening extra hard. Normally, he looks around the room, so he is easily distracted. Lying down and covering his eyes helped him concentrate on what she was saying.

13 Analogous to the physical alignment that women and men take in conversation is their topical alignment. The girls in my study tended to talk at length about one topic, but the boys tended to jump from topic to topic. The second-grade girls exchanged stories about people they knew. The second-grade boys teased, told jokes, noticed things in the room and talked about finding games to play. The sixth-grade girls talked about problems with a mutual friend. The sixth-grade boys talked about 55 different topics, none of which extended over more than a few turns.

Listening to Body Language

14 Switching topics is another habit that gives women the impression men aren't listening, especially if they switch to a topic about themselves. But the evidence of the 10th-grade boys in my study indicates otherwise. The 10th-grade boys sprawled across their chairs with bodies parallel and eyes straight ahead, rarely looking at each other. They looked as if they were riding in a car, staring out the windshield. But they were talking about their feelings. One boy was upset because a girl had told him he had a drinking problem, and the other was feeling alienated from all his friends.

15   Now, when a girl told a friend about a problem, the friend responded by asking probing questions and expressing agreement and understanding. But the boys dismissed each other's problems. Todd assured Richard that his drinking was "no big problem" because "sometimes you're funny when you're off your butt." And when Todd said he felt left out, Richard responded, "Why should you? You know more people than me."

16   Women perceived such responses as belittling and unsupportive. But the boys seemed satisfied with them. Whereas women reassure each other by implying, "You shouldn't feel bad because I've had similar experiences," men do so by implying, "You shouldn't feel bad because your problems aren't so bad."

17   There are even simpler reasons for women's impression that men don't listen. Linguist Lynette Hirschman found that women make more listener-noise, such as "mhm," "uhuh," and "yeah," to show "I'm with you." Men, she found, more often give silent attention. Women who expect a stream of listener-noise interpret silent attention as no attention at all.

18   Women's conversational habits are as frustrating to men as men's are to women. Men who expect silent attention interpret a stream of listener-noise as overreaction or impatience. Also, when women talk to each other in a close, comfortable setting, they often overlap, finish each other's sentences and anticipate what the other is about to say. This practice, which I call "participatory listenership," is often perceived by men as interruption, intrusion and lack of attention.

19   A parallel difference caused a man to complain about his wife, "She just wants to talk about her own point of view. If I show her another view, she gets mad at me." When most women talk to each other, they assume a conversationalist's job is to express agreement and support. But many men see their conversational duty as pointing out the other side of an argument. This is heard as disloyalty by women, and refusal to offer the requisite support. It is not that women don't want to see other points of view, but that they prefer them phrased as suggestions and inquiries rather than as direct challenges.

20   In his book *Fighting for Life*, Walter Ong points out that men use "agonistic" or warlike, oppositional formats to do almost anything; thus discussion becomes debate, and conversation a competitive sport. In contrast, women see conversation as a ritual means of establishing rapport. If Jane tells a problem and June says she has a similar one, they walk away feeling closer to each other. But this attempt at establishing rapport can backfire when used with men. Men take too literally women's ritual "troubles talk," just as women mistake men's ritual challenges for real attack.

The Sounds of Silence

21   These differences begin to clarify why women and men have such different expectations about communication in marriage. For women, talk creates intimacy. Marriage is an orgy of closeness: you can tell your feelings and thoughts, and still be loved. Their greatest fear is being pushed away. But men live in a hierarchical world, where talk maintains independence and status. They are on guard to protect themselves from being put down and pushed around.

22   This explains the paradox of the talkative man who said of his silent wife, "She's the talker." In the public setting of a guest lecture, he felt challenged to show his intelligence and display his understanding of the lecture. But at home, where he has nothing to prove and no one to defend against, he is free to remain silent. For his wife, being home means she is free from the worry that something she says might offend someone, or spark disagreement, or appear to be showing off; at home she is free to talk.

23   The communication problems that endanger marriage can't be fixed by mechanical engineering. They require a new conceptual framework about the role of talk in human relationships. Many of the psychological explanations that have become second nature may not be helpful, because they tend to blame either women (for not being assertive enough) or men (for not being in touch with their feelings). A sociolinguistic approach by which male-female conversation is seen as cross-cultural communication allows us to understand the problem and forge solutions without blaming either party.

24   Once the problem is understood, improvement comes naturally, as it did to the young woman and her boyfriend who seemed to go to sleep when she wanted to talk. Previously, she had accused him of not listening, and he had refused to change his behavior, since that would be admitting fault. But then she learned about and explained to him the differences in women's and men's habitual ways of aligning themselves in conversation. The next time she told him she wanted to talk, he began, as usual, by lying down and covering his eyes. When the familiar negative reaction bubbled up, she reassured herself that he really was listening. But then he sat up and looked at her. Thrilled she asked why. He said, "You like me to look at you when we talk, so I'll try to do it." Once he saw their differences as cross-cultural rather than right and wrong, he independently altered his behavior.

25   Women who feel abandoned and deprived when their husbands won't listen to or report daily news may be happy to discover their husbands trying to adapt once they understand the place of small talk in women's relationships. But if their husbands don't adapt, the women may still be comforted that for men, this is not a failure of intimacy. Accepting the difference, the wives may

look to their friends or family for that kind of talk. And husbands who can't provide it shouldn't feel their wives have made unreasonable demands. Some couples will still decide to divorce, but at least their decisions will be based on realistic expectations.

26   In these times of resurgent ethnic conflicts, the world desperately needs cross-cultural understanding. Like charity, successful cross-cultural communication should begin at home.

Understanding Meaning

1. What thesis is Tannen supporting in this essay?
2. What does Tannen say causes communication problems in so many marriages?
3. Explain the different perceptions of communication that men bring to marriage as opposed to those that women bring.
4. What does Tannen believe causes the different perceptions of communication that men and women bring to marriage?
5. How do men and women reveal this difference even through their body language?
6. *CRITICAL THINKING.* Is what Tannen says about men's and women's communication borne out by your experience? Explain.

Evaluating Strategy

1. Instead of saying everything she has to say about women and then turning to men, or vice versa (the subject-by-subject method), Tannen weaves discussion of both genders throughout the piece. Explain more specifically the point-by-point organizational pattern that she uses. Do the headings help?
2. *BLENDING THE MODES.* Where in the essay does Tannen make use of cause/effect?
3. Why does Tannen feel that male-female communication is a type of cross-cultural communication? How is this argument an additional use of comparison/contrast?
4. How does Tannen establish the authority of those whom she cites in building her case?

Appreciating Language

1. What is the effect of Tannen's use of the first person (*I*)? What gives her the authority to write on this particular subject?
2. Tannen speaks with authority, but does she use words that are not familiar to you? In other words, does she use a lot of technical jargon from her field that most people not in her field would not understand?
3. Give some examples of where Tannen smoothly introduces information from other sources while at the same time establishing the authority of the sources she is citing.

Writing Suggestions

1. Write an essay in which you explain how teenagers today have been socialized to expect a certain type of male conversation and a different type of female conversation from their peers.
2. *COLLABORATIVE WRITING.* Work with a group of students and select an upcoming television program (not a comedy) and analyze the body language based on gender. Tape the program for reference if you can. Do the characters use body language the way Tannen describes when talking one on one? Discuss your observations with members of the group. Select key scenes to watch and discuss with other students.
3. Write an essay in which you either agree or disagree with Tannen's claim that men and women expect different things out of a conversation with a member of the opposite sex.
4. Analyze the current styles of dress among teens and young adults. Do the styles selected by females seem to send a different message than those selected by males? Explain.

MICHAEL ZIELENZIGER

Michael Zielenziger (1955–) received a bachelor's degree from Princeton University and attended Stanford University for postgraduate studies. He is a reporter for the Knight-Ridder/Tribune News Service. Based in Tokyo, he has published numerous articles on Asian economic and political affairs. In addition, he has commented on a wide variety of social and cultural issues, ranging from Japanese wedding customs to Tokyo nightlife.

Black Is Beautiful: Tokyo Style

CONTEXT: *As you read this article, consider the media images of African Americans distributed throughout the world. Does popular culture provide realistic representations of blacks and other minorities?*

1   Tokyo—They're bouncing to hip-hop music at health clubs, boogying all night to rhythm and blues at the Soul Train Cafe. Women are curling their hair into Afro style haircuts—called "wafferu" (wafe) hair—while their boyfriends are growing goatees or taking to tanning rooms to darken their complexion.

2   Suddenly black is very, very beautiful for some of Tokyo's trendiest youth.

3   From dance parties in Roppongi to cutting-edge videos on television, from rising demand for porkpie hats to a rush for "gangsta" fashion, a new focus on African-American music and culture is giving voice to a strain of rebelliousness in young Japanese, confronting the most serious economic stagnation in 50 years.

4   "When I listen to this music, I don't have to think," explained Takako Yamamoto, 20, as she danced with a boyfriend at a Tokyo soul club. "I don't have to deal with work or stress. I can just be free. Black people and black music are totally cool."

5   "It's a way of telling people you don't want to be part of the large corporate lifestyle," said Minako Suzuki Wilder, who admires the new black scene. "A lot of people in their 20s are not into working at old-fashioned companies, so they get into the black music and the hip-hop dancing, getting frizzy hair or an Afro haircut.

6   "It's new to us and it seems fun. People like the way the music helps you work out your stress."

7   Strains of black culture have long existed in Japan, often carried here by African-American soldiers who decide to stay on. Jazz bars permeated in the 1950s and black baseball players often have become popular.

8   But now a new generation of black culture has entered the Japanese mainstream.

9   The most obvious sign: the appearance last month of a new beer called "Dunk," whose name alone connotes the German word "dunkel," for dark beer, with allusions to basketball players jamming the ball through the hoop.

10   Dunk advertisements, which now plaster Tokyo's subways, employ three sequined-studded, sashaying Motown-style singers and a Japanese entertainer, Masayuki Suzuki, most noted for his efforts to look African-American. During the 1980s, Suzuki dressed in blackface and white gloves to belt out soul songs for a group known as "Shanels."

11   "We didn't need to have a focus group to see whether black is cool," said Kiyoshi Oguri, marketing researcher for Asahi Brewery, manufacturers of Dunk. "But when we see black people playing ball on TV, not only basketball but also on entertainment programs, we could see that would be the right focus for us. We didn't intentionally focus on black culture, but certainly there is a recognition that black is cool.

12   "We knew that black things were 'kakko-ii' (cool). It's hard to explain the reason that it's 'kakko-ii,' but we know it is there."

13   However, observers note that because the relatively insulated Japanese have not been exposed to African-American culture, they tend to go wild over stereotypes.

14   "They may be interested in the trappings, but really their interest in African-American culture is completely superficial," said Kako Kawachi, who teaches women's and African-American studies at the prestigious Waseda University.

15   She dismisses the black fashion trend as a fad that has not brought new students into her classes.

16   "It's very shallow," she said.

17   Still, the surge in interest in things black is creating opportunities for African-Americans in Japan.

18   "Really, it's paradise over here," said Thomas Paul, a hip-hop dance instructor and promoter, who earns nearly $4,000 a month teaching spin moves and twists at a health club. "People think we're really exotic, and most are really open to learning about the real hip-hop scene. A lot of folks come to check out my class just to experience real black culture."

19   His classes are a sea of twisting arms and sweat-drenched T-shirts as 20- and 30-year old Japanese, predominately women, try to mimic Paul's dance-steps and twirls. "Twist! 'Mawatte!' (Turn!) 'Tatte!' (Stand!)," Paul shouts at his students as they attempt to master his complex choreography.

20   While there aren't many blacks in Japan, those who land here find themselves among the most exotic, erotic and sought-after foreigners ever to set foot in this homogeneous and somewhat insulated island nation.

21   "You can feel the difference in the air," said jazz saxophone star Branford Marsalis, who recently concluded a three-week tour of Japan with his quartet. "When I first came to Japan eight years ago, people stared at you and thought you were strange. They really kept their distance and were sort of standoffish.

22   "But now, people are totally into what we are doing," he explained after a set at Tokyo's Blue Note jazz cafe. "They really listen to the music, and after the shows, the people really want to meet and talk to you.

23   "The attitude has completely changed, and it's really great."

24   In a nation that consciously encourages its young people to forge cohesive group identity, Japan always has produced its share of rebels who shun the corporate blue suits. Twenty-something "greasers" with slicked-back, duck-tail haircuts and leather jackets regularly dance on the weekends in Yoyogi Park. The Varsity shop sells cheerleader costumes. Reggae bars and salsa clubs beckoned the affluent and adventurous seeking a good time.

25   But the black trend, researchers say, signifies a clear disenchantment with the rigidity and lack of individual expression in Japan.

26   "In Japanese society, you don't have many options; society is quite inflexible," said Akiko Togawa, a market researcher for Dentsu Eye. "Most young Japanese don't see any successful entrepreneurs around them in Japan.

27   "So when they see black people who have made it, despite the discrimination in America, they see people who have successfully asserted their individual identity. So in a way, it's a revolt against traditional Japanese culture."

28   Valerie Koehn, a Tokyo-based designer and writer, says the rebellious quality of hip-hop and rap music is what is generating more interest in African-Americans and their culture. "It's the young people saying 'We don't care what our parents did or what society demands of us. We don't have to do that.' It's totally in your face."

29   Toshiaki Koike, 34, an executive with a debt-ridden construction company, says he prefers going to black music bars because "there's more energy. Times aren't good right now," he said, over the strains of a rap song at the Soul Train Cafe. "But here I can get great energy from the music."

30   His friend Yamamoto said she really likes rap music and would love to meet more African-Americans. But, as Kawachi, the black studies professor, indicated, this new fascination with black people might be more style than substance and does not necessarily mean all cultural biases have been conquered.

31   "I don't think I'd want to date one," Yamamoto said of African-Americans. "I'd be a little afraid."

Understanding Meaning

1. According to Zielenziger, why do young Japanese embrace hip-hop music and "gangsta" fashion? What does it represent to them? Why is black "cool"?
2. How does Zielenziger say Japanese attitudes towards African Americans have changed in the last decade?
3. What images of African Americans seem to have been exported to Japan?
4. In Zielenziger's opinion, how did Japan's recent recession influence the popularity of black culture?
5. *CRITICAL THINKING.* American movies and television programs are viewed worldwide. Are people in other countries likely to develop distorted images of Americans?

Evaluating Strategy

1. Zielenziger includes numerous quotations in his essay. How effectively does he organize them?
2. Do the comments by Kako Kawachi, who dismisses the Japanese interest in black culture as a shallow fad, form an implied thesis?
3. How effective is the last quotation? What impact does it have on readers? What does it reveal about Japanese attitudes towards African Americans?

Appreciating Language

1. This is a news article, which is written to be skimmed rather than read. How do word choice, sentence structure, and paragraph length affect its readability?
2. What do Japanese words like "wafferu" for "wafe" and "kako-ii" for "cool" suggest about the influence of English in Japan?

Writing Suggestions

1. Write a brief essay outlining your view of the Japanese, based solely on their media image. How are the Japanese represented in movies and television programs? What are the positive and negative stereotypes?
2. *COLLABORATIVE WRITING.* Discuss this article with a group of students. Note members' observations and reactions. Work together to draft a short statement analyzing the way in which U.S. popular culture influences world opinion about Americans.